GRAPHIS PHOTO 89

GRAPHIS PHOTO 89

The International Annual of Photography
Das Internationale Jahrbuch der Photographie
Le Répertoire International de la Photographie

Edited by/Herausgegeben von/Réalisé par
B. Martin Pedersen

Publisher and Creative Director: B. Martin Pedersen
Assistant Editors: Heinke Jenssen, Annette Crandall
Designers: Martin Byland, Udi Nadiv
Photographer: Walter Zuber

Graphis Press Corp., Zurich (Switzerland)

GRAPHIS PUBLICATIONS

GRAPHIS, International bi-monthly journal of graphic art and photography

GRAPHIS DESIGN, The international annual on design and illustration

GRAPHIS PHOTO, The international annual of photography

GRAPHIS POSTER, The international annual of poster art

GRAPHIS PACKAGING, An international survey of packaging design

GRAPHIS DIAGRAM, The graphic visualization of abstract, technical and statistical facts and functions

GRAPHIS COVERS, An anthology of all GRAPHIS covers from 1944–86 with artists' short biographies
  and indexes of all GRAPHIS issues

GRAPHIS ANNUAL REPORTS, An international compilation of the best designed annual reports

POSTERS MADE POSSIBLE BY A GRANT FROM MOBIL, A collection of 250 international posters commissioned by Mobil
  and selected by the Poster Society

GRAPHIS-PUBLIKATIONEN

GRAPHIS, Die internationale Zweimonatszeitschrift für Graphik und Photographie

GRAPHIS DESIGN, Das internationale Jahrbuch über Design und Illustration

GRAPHIS PHOTO, Das internationale Jahrbuch der Photographie

GRAPHIS POSTER, Das internationale Jahrbuch der Plakatkunst

GRAPHIS PACKUNGEN, Ein internationaler Überblick der Packungsgestaltung

GRAPHIS DIAGRAM, Die graphische Darstellung abstrakter, technischer und statistischer Daten und Fakten

GRAPHIS COVERS, Eine Sammlung aller GRAPHIS-Umschläge von 1944–86 mit Informationen über die Künstler
  und Inhaltsübersichten aller Ausgaben der Zeitschrift GRAPHIS

GRAPHIS ANNUAL REPORTS, Ein internationaler Überblick der Gestaltung von Jahresberichten

POSTERS MADE POSSIBLE BY A GRANT FROM MOBIL, Eine Sammlung von 250 internationalen Plakaten, von Mobil
  in Auftrag gegeben und von der Poster Society ausgewählt

PUBLICATIONS GRAPHIS

GRAPHIS, La revue bimestrielle internationale d'arts graphiques et de la photographie

GRAPHIS DESIGN, Le répertoire international de la communication visuelle

GRAPHIS PHOTO, Le répertoire international de la photographie

GRAPHIS POSTER, Le répertoire international de l'art de l'affiche

GRAPHIS EMBALLAGES, Le répertoire international des formes de l'emballage

GRAPHIS DIAGRAM, La représentation graphique de faits et données abstraits, techniques et statistiques

GRAPHIS COVERS, Recueil de toutes les couvertures de GRAPHIS de 1944–86 avec des notices biographiques
  des artistes et le sommaire de tous les numéros du magazine GRAPHIS.

GRAPHIS ANNUAL REPORTS, Panorama international du design de rapports annuels d'entreprises

POSTERS MADE POSSIBLE BY A GRANT FROM MOBIL, Une collection de 250 affiches internationales commandées par Mobil
  et choisies par la Poster Society

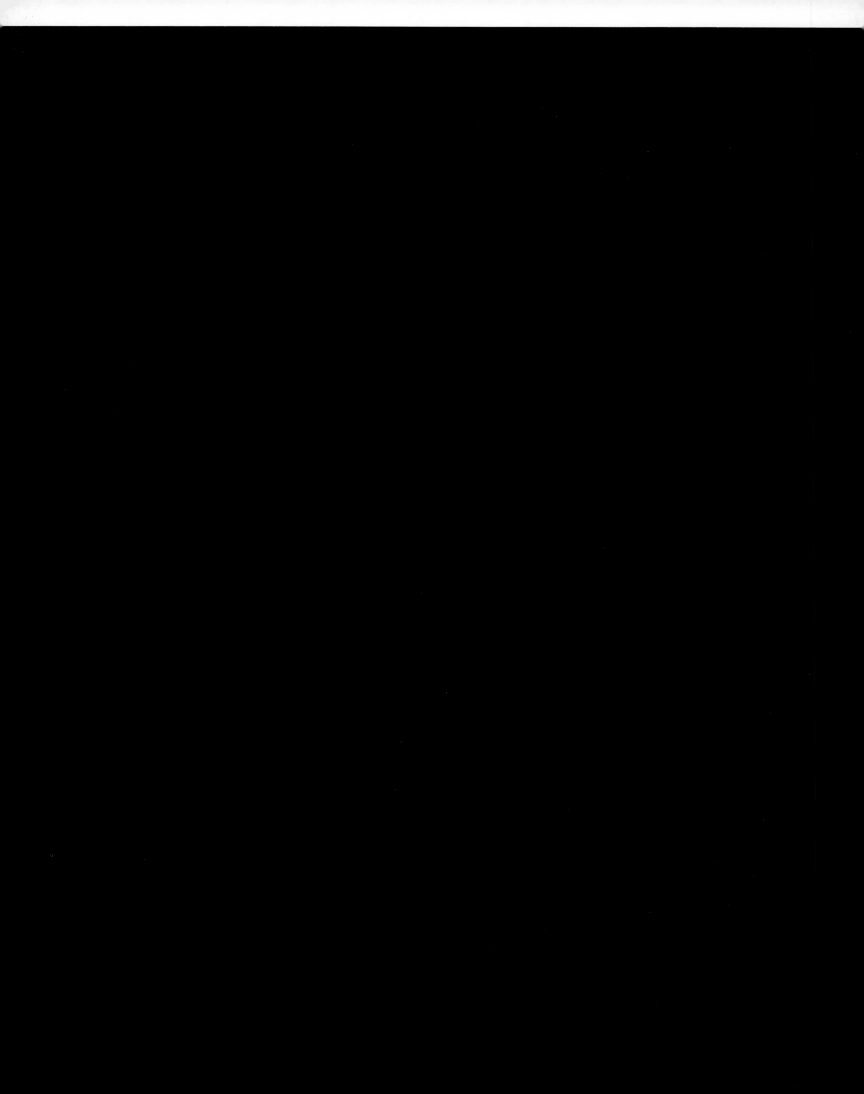

ABBREVIATIONS

Australia	AUS
Austria	AUT
Belgium	BEL
Canada	CAN
Czechoslovakia	CSR
Denmark	DEN
France	FRA
Germany (West)	GER
Great Britain	GBR
Italy	ITA
Japan	JPN
Korea	KOR
Netherlands	NLD
Norway	NOR
Spain	SPA
Sweden	SWE
Switzerland	SWI
Turkey	TUR
USA	USA

ABKÜRZUNGEN

Australien	AUS
Belgien	BEL
Dänemark	DEN
Deutschland (BRD)	GER
Frankreich	FRA
Grossbritannien	GBR
Italien	ITA
Japan	JPN
Kanada	CAN
Korea	KOR
Niederlande	NLD
Norwegen	NOR
Österreich	AUT
Schweden	SWE
Schweiz	SWI
Spanien	SPA
Tschechoslowakei	CSR
Türkei	TUR
USA	USA

ABRÉVIATIONS

Allemagne (R.F.A.)	GER
Australie	AUS
Autriche	AUT
Belgique	BEL
Canada	CAN
Corée	KOR
Danemark	DEN
Espagne	SPA
Etats-Unis	USA
France	FRA
Grande-Bretagne	GBR
Italie	ITA
Japon	JPN
Norvège	NOR
Pays-Bas	NLD
Suède	SWE
Suisse	SWI
Tchécoslovaquie	CSR
Turquie	TUR

REMARKS

■ We extend our heartfelt thanks to contributors throughout the world who have made it possible for us to publish a wide and international spectrum of the best work in this field.

■ Entry instructions may be requested at:
Graphis Press Corp., Dufourstrasse 107,
8008 Zurich, Switzerland

ANMERKUNGEN

■ Unser herzlicher Dank gilt den Einsendern aus aller Welt, die es uns durch ihre Beiträge möglich gemacht haben, ein breites, internationales Spektrum der besten Arbeiten zu veröffentlichen.

■ Teilnahmebedingungen:
Graphis Verlag AG, Dufourstrasse 107,
8008 Zurich, Schweiz

ANNOTATIONS

■ Toute notre reconnaissance va aux designers du monde entier dont les envois nous ont permis de constituer un vaste panorama international des meilleurs travaux.

■ Modalités d'envoi de travaux:
Editions Graphis SA, Dufourstrasse 107,
8008 Zurich, Suisse

JAY MAISEL

It's easy to criticize or praise, but difficult to solve any of the photographic industry's problems. It's unnecessary to go into detail about the major changes which have taken place in the last 35 years. Most of us know that cameras and reproduction quality have improved by quantum leaps. We are also aware of the proliferation of fine photographers on a worldwide basis.

Sadly, we also note that the quest for excellence which was a hallmark of the '60's and '70's has been replaced by a mania for bottom line results. Too often we find ourselves in the hands of those who "know the price of everything and the value of nothing".

There is still original work being created, but a "copycat mentality" is epidemic. Art directors now have a plethora of source books in which they can find a great shot and then ask someone else to do it cheaper. We also know that the exponential increase in the number of photographers has created an imbalance in the law of supply and demand – one law that will never change.

In many annuals you will see excellent work, much of which is self-promotion. The photograph is the primary message and the photographer has a greater-than-normal say in how the finished piece appears. When the designer's or art director's authority is unchecked, the "fine hand of the designer" can egocentrically overshadow the aim of the final product. I don't exempt photographers from this fault (I want to offend all groups equally) because they too often subvert a concept to a trendy style or gimmick.

Instead of continuing in this negative manner, I would like to talk about some favorite people I've worked for and what I would look for if I were in their position.

My favorite art directors and designers are not necessarily the ones with the most money. They may have some bucks to play with but that's not their best feature. They may accompany me on a shoot or they may stay away. Either way is okay, but whatever they do, they have faith in me to do my job. They have confidence in their ability to impart the particulars of the assignment and, having done that, they're able to delegate the rest. They understand that I have a passion for my work and they try not to dilute it.

In a business where there are not only art directors, but creative directors, copywriters, account executives, art buyers, media buyers, communications directors, production people, and clients, the great art directors speak to me in a clear voice. They have managed to create a concept and steer it through all of the above while keeping it pure. That idea and its final form using the photograph in relation to type and design is their critical contribution of the work.

Whether they come along on location or not, during the shoot they may feel like a midwife during the fourth month of pregnancy – necessary, but not for a while yet. It is at this time that my favorite art directors and designers are at the top of their form. They observe, they tell me if I'm doing something stupid or if I'm headed in the wrong direction. They don't try to tell me exactly how to do this or that because in their initial charge to me they've conveyed what they want and they see that I'm desperately trying to do it for them. When I finally run out of ideas or energy and ask them for their input, they either come up with another brilliant idea or just say those wonderful words "I think you've got it". At which point, being insecure and "still crazy after all these years", I try to go back and do it yet another way.

The most important thing about my ideal creative person is that they've done their homework. In their client presentation they've explained that the comp is a stepping stone to creativity, not an end in itself. They make the client realize that an idea on paper may be improved upon in the field.

If I were an art director my ideal photographers would be the ones with a passion for their work, to whom photographs are precious, who care for them like children. They're not the ones who sell their work cheap or outright, on buyouts or work for hire. I figure if they sell cheap or fail to protect their rights, they simply don't have much respect for their work. If they did, they wouldn't put such a low price on it or give it up so easily.

Of course my favorite photographers work their butts off for me. Beyond that, they're ethical and never abuse the use of pictures they take for me. They would never ever sell them to my client's competition and never run them – even in their own publicity – before I have. If I tell them my project is confidential, they respect that. If I give them an assignment to shoot something one way and they find something better, they have the guts and initiative to shoot it both ways.

They have faith in themselves and don't worry me with problems of the job. I've hired them to worry for the two for us.

They are obsessive about their work. It isn't just a job for them, they love to do it. Conversely, if they aren't inspired by the job, they don't do it with feet-dragging and no enthusiasm, they recommend someone who would be right for the project. If they take the job, they can bring it in within the budget outlined before shooting started. They are incredibly responsible and understand that my ass is on the line if they screw up; there are no acceptable excuses when it's time to turn in the job.

Finally, great work starts with great clients. The art director, designer, client, and photographer must avoid the danger of their relationship becoming adversarial. All must be motivated by a burning desire never to be boring, by a commitment to make something wonderful, exciting, and beautiful.

We only have a few moments to make an impression. Our primary mission is to keep the reader from turning the page. What we do must leave people wiser, happier, in some way enriched by the experience.

To give something of value for the reader's time is not only ethical and moral, it's good business in relation to good design and it pays off.

Jay Maisel is one of photography's most outstanding – and outspoken – talents. Born in Brooklyn, New York, he studied painting at New York's Cooper Union and holds a Bachelor of Fine Arts degree from Yale University. His photographic studies came under the tutelage of Herbert Matter and Alexi Brodovitch, among others. A freelance photographer since 1954, Maisel's work is held in numerous private and corporate collections, and has been widely published in books and magazines throughout the world. The winner of many prestigious awards, he is the recipient of two Gold Medals from the Art Directors' Club of New York (in 1986 and 1987) and was named the ASMP's "Photographer of the Year" for 1986. In addition to his photography, Maisel lectures extensively and conducts several annual workshops.

JAY MAISEL

Kritik oder Lob wäre einfach, aber eine Lösung für die Probleme der photographischen Industrie zu finden ist schwer. Es ist nicht nötig, auf Einzelheiten der Veränderungen einzugehen, die in den letzten 35 Jahren stattgefunden haben. Die meisten von uns wissen, dass in der Entwicklung der Kameras und der Reproduktionsqualität grosse Fortschritte gemacht wurden. Wir wissen auch, dass es überall auf der Welt immer mehr ausgezeichnete Photographen gibt.

Traurig ist allerdings, dass das Bemühen um Qualität, das die 60er und 70er Jahre kennzeichnete, einem rein materiellen Denken Platz gemacht hat. Nur allzuoft sind wir jenen ausgeliefert, die «den Preis von allem und den Wert von gar nichts» kennen.

Originalität findet man noch immer in der Photographie, aber es grassiert eine «Kopier»-Epidemie. Art Direktoren arbeiten mit zahllosen Handbüchern, in denen sie manche hervorragende Aufnahme finden können, und dann beauftragen sie einfach jemanden, das gleiche zu machen, aber natürlich billiger.

Wir wissen auch, dass durch die ungeheuer gestiegene Anzahl von Photographen das Gleichgewicht von Angebot und Nachfrage aus den Fugen geraten ist – von einem Gesetz, das immer gültig sein wird.

In vielen Büchern werden Sie hervorragende Arbeiten sehen, viele davon sind Eigenwerbung. Die Aufnahme ist hier die Hauptbotschaft, und die Entscheidung über ihre Präsentation liegt in diesem Fall in den Händen des Photographen. Wenn Graphik-Designer oder Art Direktoren zuviel zu sagen haben, kann die «sensible Hand des Graphikers» ein solches Übergewicht bekommen, dass die ursprüngliche Aussage völlig verlorengeht. Ich nehme Photographen hier nicht aus (ich will alle Gruppen in gleichem Masse treffen), weil sie nur allzuoft ein Konzept zugunsten eines modischen Stils oder eines Gags verraten. Doch statt so negativ fortzufahren, möchte ich über einige Leute reden, die ich mag und für die ich gearbeitet habe, und ich möchte sagen, was ich an ihrer Stelle tun würde.

Die Art Direktoren und Graphik-Designer, die mir am liebsten sind, haben nicht unbedingt am meisten Geld zur Verfügung. Sie haben unter Umständen ein gewisses Budget, mit dem sie spielen können, aber das ist es nicht, was sie auszeichnet. Sie können bei den Aufnahmen dabei sein oder nicht. Beides ist in Ordnung, aber was immer sie machen, sie haben Vertrauen in mich und meine Arbeit. Sie trauen sich selbst zu, das besondere Anliegen eines Auftrags erklären zu können, und nachdem sie das getan haben, sind sie in der Lage, den Rest zu delegieren. Sie wissen, was meine Arbeit für mich bedeutet, und sie versuchen nicht, sie zu verwässern.

Wenn es in einer Firma nicht nur Art Direktoren gibt, sondern auch Kreativ-Direktoren, Texter, Kundenberater, Art Buyer, Media Buyer, Kommunikations-Direktoren, Produktionsleute und Kunden, dann spricht ein guter Art Direktor eine klare, eindeutige Sprache. Es ist ihnen gelungen, ein Konzept auszuarbeiten und es unbeschadet durch sämtliche soeben erwähnte Instanzen zu bringen. Diese Idee und ihre endgültige Ausführung, bei der die Aufnahme in Relation zu Typographie und Design eingesetzt wird, ist ihr Anteil an der Arbeit.

Sollten sie bei den Aufnahmen dabei sein, so werden sie sich wahrscheinlich wie eine Hebamme im vierten Monat einer Schwangerschaft fühlen – sie werden gebraucht, aber es wird noch eine Weile dauern. In dieser Phase sind die Art Direktoren und Graphik-Designer, die mir am liebsten sind, in Höchstform. Sie beobachten, sie sagen mir, wenn ich etwas Dummes mache oder in die falsche Richtung gehe. Sie versuchen nicht, mir zu sagen, wie ich dieses oder jenes machen muss, weil sie mir bereits zu Beginn des Auftrags alles Nötige gesagt haben und weil sie sehen, dass ich alles daransetze, das Richtige für sie zu tun. Wenn mir schliesslich überhaupt keine Ideen mehr kommen und ich sie um Rat bitte, haben sie entweder eine ganz ausgezeichnete Idee oder sie sagen einfach die wunderbaren Worte «Ich glaube, jetzt ist es gut». An diesem Punkt mache ich mich nochmal an die Arbeit und versuche noch etwas anderes, weil ich unsicher und «nach all diesen Jahren noch immer verrückt» bin.

Bei meiner Idealvorstellung einer kreativen Person ist es am wichtigsten, dass diese ihre Hausaufgaben gemacht hat. Bei der Präsentation hat sie dem Kunden klargemacht, dass der Entwurf ein Schritt zur Kreativität ist und nicht eine abgeschlossene Sache. Sie überzeugt den Kunden, dass eine Idee auf dem Papier bei der Umsetzung noch besser herauskommen kann.

Wäre ich Art Direktor, würden Photographen, die ganz in ihrer Arbeit aufgehen, für die Photographien etwas Kostbares sind und die sie wie ihre Kinder behandeln, meiner Idealvorstellung entsprechen. Nicht dazu gehören jene, die ihre Arbeit billig oder ohne Bedenken verkaufen, die unterbieten oder die einfach alles machen würden. Wenn sie sich billig verkaufen oder ihre Rechte nicht verteidigen, stelle ich mir vor, dass sie keine grosse Achtung vor ihrer Arbeit haben. Denn wenn sie es hätten, würden sie keinen so niedrigen Preis dafür verlangen und sich nicht so leicht davon trennen.

Natürlich geben meine Lieblingsphotographen ihr Letztes für mich. Darüber hinaus haben sie eine Berufsethik und missbrauchen die Aufnahmen, die sie für mich machen, nie für andere Zwecke. Sie würden sie niemals der Konkurrenz meines Kunden verkaufen und sie nicht veröffentlichen – auch nicht als Eigenwerbung – bevor ich es nicht getan habe. Wenn ich ihnen sage, dass mein Projekt vertraulich ist, respektieren sie das. Wenn ich sie beauftrage, ein Photo auf eine bestimmte Art zu machen, sie aber eine bessere Idee haben, so haben sie den Mut und die Initiative, beide Wege auszuprobieren.

Sie haben Selbstvertrauen und belasten mich nicht mit ihren Problemen bei der Arbeit. Ich habe ihnen den Auftrag gegeben, damit sie das Kopfzerbrechen für uns beide übernehmen.

Sie sind von ihrer Arbeit besessen. Für sie ist es nicht ein Job, sie lieben ihre Arbeit. Auf der anderen Seite quälen sie sich nicht ohne jegliche Begeisterung mit einem Auftrag ab, der ihnen nicht liegt, sondern sie empfehlen jemanden, der ihnen geeignet erscheint. Wenn sie den Auftrag annehmen, halten sie sich an das vereinbarte Budget. Sie sind unglaublich verantwortungsbewusst und verstehen, dass ich dran bin, wenn sie Mist bauen und dass es keine akzeptable Entschuldigung für das Nichteinhalten des Termins gibt.

Schliesslich sei noch gesagt, dass gute Arbeit mit guten Kunden beginnt. Art Direktor, Graphik-Designer, Kunde und Photograph dürfen nicht zu Gegnern werden. Sie alle müssen von dem brennenden Wunsch beseelt sein, nie etwa Langweiliges zu machen, sondern etwas Wunderbares, Aufregendes und Schönes.

Wir haben nur ein paar Augenblicke, um eine Wirkung zu erzielen. Unser grösstes Anliegen ist, den Betrachter davon abzuhalten, die Seite gleich umzuschlagen. Unsere Arbeit soll die Leute klüger, glücklicher und um ein Erlebnis reicher machen.

Es ist nicht nur ethisch und moralisch, dem Leser für seine Zeit etwas von Wert zu geben, es ist auch ein gutes Geschäft zusammen mit gutem Design, und es zahlt sich aus.

Jay Maisel ist einer der grössten zeitgenössischen Photographen -und jemand, der sagt, was er denkt. Er wurde in Brooklyn, New York, geboren und studierte Malerei an der Cooper Union, New York. An der Yale University schloss er als «Bachelor of Fine Arts» ab. In der Photographie zählen Herbert Matter und Alexi Brodovitch zu seinen Lehrmeistern. Seit 1954 arbeitet er als freier Photograph. Seine Aufnahmen befinden sich in zahlreichen Sammlungen von Privatleuten und Firmen, und sie wurden immer wieder in Büchern und Zeitschriften in der ganzen Welt gezeigt. Er hat für seine Arbeit viele bedeutende Auszeichnungen erhalten, darunter zwei Goldmedaillen des Art Directors' Club von New York (1986 und 1987), und von der ASMP wurde er 1986 zum «Photographen des Jahres» gewählt. Neben seiner photographischen Arbeit hält Jay Maisel Vorlesungen und veranstaltet jährlich Workshops.

JAY MAISEL

Si l'éloge et la critique sont choses faciles, plus difficile est la solution des problèmes que rencontre l'industrie photographique. Il n'est guère nécessaire de revenir en détail sur les transformations importantes intervenues au cours des 35 dernières années. La plupart d'entre nous sont bien conscients de ce que les appareils photo et la qualité de la reproduction ont progressé par de véritables sauts quantiques. Nous réalisons de même que la photographie de haut niveau a connu une expansion sans précédent dans le monde entier.

Malheureusement nous notons aussi que la recherche de l'excellence qui caractérisait les années 60 et 70 s'est muée en une obsession maniaque du chiffre d'affaires. Trop souvent, nous sommes livrés pieds et mains liés à ceux qui «connaissent le prix de toute chose, mais ne savent la valeur de rien».

Des travaux originaux continuent certes de voir le jour, mais une mentalité de pisse-copie fait actuellement rage. Les directeurs artistiques ont désormais une pléthore de documentations à disposition où ils peuvent repérer des photos exceptionnelles, pour charger un tâcheron d'en faire un imitation à bas prix.

Nous savons aussi que l'augmentation exponentielle du nombre des photographes a déséquilibré la loi de l'offre et de la demande – une loi d'airain, qui ne changera jamais.

Dans nombre d'annuels, on trouvera d'excellents travaux dont une grande partie sert à l'autopromotion de leurs auteurs. La photo y constitue le message primordial, et le photographe a une part plus importante que d'ordinaire dans son élaboration. Lorsque l'autorité du designer ou du directeur artistique ne rencontre aucun obstacle, «la main admirable du créatif» peut, de manière égocentrique, recouvrir de son ombre le but tracé au produit fini. Si je n'exempte pas les photographes (je tiens à offenser un groupe autant que l'autre), c'est qu'ils ont trop souvent tendance à dévier subversivement un concept donné en prouesse de style éphémère ou en astuce cousue de fil blanc. Voilà pour les constats négatifs. J'aimerais maintenant vous parler de quelques gens que j'aime bien, avec qui j'ai travaillé et imaginer ce que je ferais à leur place.

Les directeurs artistiques et les designers que je préfère ne sont pas nécessairement ceux qui ont le plus d'argent à dépenser. S'il leur arrive d'avoir quelques sous de trop pour s'amuser avec, ce n'est certes pas là leur trait le plus avantageux. Il leur arrive de m'accompagner pour une prise de vues ou de s'abstenir. Chacune de ces deux démarches me convient. Quoi qu'ils fassent, ils me font confiance pour mon travail. Ils sont également confiants en ce qui concerne leur aptitude à énoncer clairement les données du problème posé et, une fois la mission définie, à déléguer tout le reste. Ils savent que j'éprouve pour mon travail une passion qu'ils évitent d'affaiblir.

Dans un secteur d'activité où il n'y a pas seulement des directeurs artistiques, mais aussi des directeurs créatifs, des rédacteurs, des responsables de budget, des acheteurs d'art, des acheteurs de médias, des directeurs de la communication, des spécialistes de la production et des clients, les grands directeurs artistiques s'adressent à moi dans un langage clair. Ils ont réussi à créer un concept et s'évertuent à lui faire passer tous les écueils representés par les personnages évoqués en en préservant la pureté. Leur contribution critique au travail en cours, c'est cette idée et la forme finale qu'elle prend en utilisant la photo en relation avec le texte et le design.

Qu'ils m'accompagnent sur le site ou non, ils risquent d'avoir pendant la prise de vues les mêmes idées qu'une sage-femme considérant une grossesse de quatre mois: elle sait que son intervention sera nécessaire, mais pas en l'état actuel des choses. C'est à ce moment-là que les directeurs artistiques et designers que j'aime bien sont au mieux de leur forme. Ils observent ce que je fais, me signalent mes erreurs ou corrigent le tir. Ils n'essaient pas de me dire avec précision ce que je dois faire ou non, puisque, dans l'énoncé de la mission, ils ont déjà défini ce qu'ils entendent obtenir et qu'ils se rendent bien compte que je fais tout mon possible de l'obtenir pour eux. Quand, pour finir, je me retrouve à court d'idées ou d'énergie et leur demande de me relancer, soit ils font jaillir une idée éblouissante, soit ils se contentent de prononcer ces mots merveilleux: «Je crois que vous y êtes». A ce moment, incertain d'avoir vraiment réussi et «toujours aussi fou après tant d'années», je risque de reprendre tout à zéro et de tenter une autre approche.

La chose la plus importante qu'il y a à dire du personnage créatif idéal, c'est qu'il a fait ce qu'il fallait faire à temps et avec compétence. Dans la présentation au client, il a pris soin d'expliquer que la composition à l'étude n'est qu'une première étape vers la créativité et non pas une fin en soi. Il a fait comprendre au client qu'une idée sur le papier peut être améliorée sur le site de la prise de vues.

Si j'étais directeur artistique, mes photographes idéals seraient ceux qui se passionnent pour leur travail, ceux pour qui les photos sont une matière précieuse dont il faut s'occuper comme d'un enfant. Ce ne seraient pas ceux qui vendent leurs travaux bon marché ou à forfait, en solde ou en louage. J'imagine que si ces gens-là se vendent à bas prix ou ne réussissent pas à protéger leurs droits, c'est qu'ils n'éprouvent guère de respect pour leurs œuvres. S'ils en éprouvaient, ils n'indiqueraient pas un prix aussi bas ni ne les livreraient aussi facilement aux acheteurs à tous crins.

Bien sûr, mes photographes favoris se crèveraient au travail pour moi. Et puis, ils observeraient une certaine éthique qui leur interdirait par exemple d'utiliser ailleurs les photos qu'ils prendraient pour mon compte. Surtout, ils ne les vendraient jamais au concurrent de mon client et ne les utiliseraient jamais – même pas pour leur propre publicité – avant que je ne l'aie fait. Si je leur disais que mon projet est confidentiel, ils respecteraient le secret. Si je les chargeais de prendre une photo d'une certaine manière et qu'ils en découvrent une meilleure, ils auraient l'intelligence et l'initiative de réaliser des prises de vues dans les deux sens.

Ils auraient confiance en eux-mêmes et ne viendraient pas m'ennuyer avec les détails du travail à effectuer. Je les engagerais précisément pour s'en occuper à ma place.

Ils seraient obsédés par leur travail. Ce ne serait pas qu'un travail à leurs yeux, ils brûleraient de le faire. A l'inverse, si la tâche ne les inspirait pas, ils renonceraient à s'en charger en traînant les pieds sans enthousiasme: ils me recommanderaient quelqu'un qui serait l'homme du boulot. S'ils acceptaient le travail, ils le réaliseraient dans le cadre du budget fixé avant la prise de vues. Ils auraient un sens aigu des responsabilités et comprendraient le tort qu'ils me feraient en me bousillant la photo. Il n'y a pas d'excuses qui tiennent quand le moment est venu de présenter des résultats.

Finalement, un travail de grande classe présuppose des clients de grande classe. Le directeur artistique, le designer, le client et le photographe doivent à tout prix éviter que leurs relations ne dégénèrent. Ils doivent être motivés par le même désir ardent de ne pas se marcher sur les pieds, de réaliser quelque chose de merveilleux, d'excitant, de superbe.

Nous ne disposons que de quelques instants pour faire impression. Notre mission essentielle consiste à empêcher le lecteur de tourner la page. Ce que nous faisons doit laisser les êtres plus sages, plus heureux, enrichis d'une façon ou d'une autre par l'expérience visuelle. Donner en échange du temps qu'investit le lecteur quelque chose qui ait de la valeur n'est pas seulement un acte éthique, moral, c'est aussi une bonne affaire en relation avec un design de qualité, et ça rapporte.

Jay Maisel est l'un des talents les plus remarquables – et les plus carrés – de l'univers de la photo. Né à Brooklyn, New York, il a étudié la peinture dans sa ville natale, à Cooper Union, et est Bachelor of Fine Arts de l'Université Yale. Ses études de photographie se sont déroulées sous l'égide de Herbert Matter et d'Alexi Brodovitch, entre autres. Etabli à son propre compte depuis 1954, Maisel a vu des œuvres intégrées dans de nombreuses collections privées et publiques. Un grand nombre d'ouvrages et d'articles de magazines lui ont été consacrés dans le monde entier. Lauréat d'une multitude de prix prestigieux, il a été récompensé entre autres par deux médailles d'or de l'Art Directors Club new-yorkais en 1986 et 1987. En 1986, il a été élu «Photographe de l'Année» par l'ASMP. Il double son travail de photographe de tournées de conférences et dirige chaque année une série d'ateliers.

MODE

PHOTOGRAPHER:
Sheila Metzner
CLIENT:
Vogue Paris
PUBLISHER:
Condé Nast SA
ART DIRECTOR:
Paul Wagner
■ 1

■ 1 Photograph of Tina
Chow, the American jewelry
designer, as published in the
Paris *Vogue.* (FRA)

■ 1 Porträtaufnahme der
amerikanischen Schmuck-
designerin Tina Chow aus
Vogue Paris. (FRA)

■ 1 Photo de la créatrice de
bijoux américaine Tina
Chow, publiée dans *Vogue*
Paris. (FRA)

PHOTOGRAPHER:
Sheila Metzner
CLIENT:
Deutsche Vogue
PUBLISHER:
Condé Nast Verlag GmbH
ART DIRECTOR:
Angelica Blechschmidt
■ 2, 3

■ 2 From an article in the
German edition of *Vogue*
entitled "Quintessence for
your Beauty". (GER)

■ 3 Brown is the theme of
this article on fashion in the
German *Vogue.* (GER)

■ 2 Aus einem Beitrag in
der deutschen *Vogue* mit
dem Titel «Quintessenz für
Ihre Schönheit». (GER)

■ 3 Die Farbe Braun ist das
Thema dieses Beitrages aus
der deutschen *Vogue.* (GER)

■ 2 Pour un article de *Vogue*
Allemagne: «Quintessence
de votre beauté». (GER)

■ 3 Le brun est le thème de
cet article dans l'édition allemande de *Vogue.* (GER)

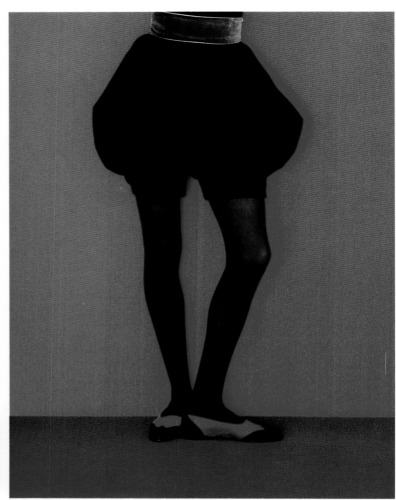

PHOTOGRAPHER:
BARRY LATEGAN
CLIENT:
VOGUE ITALIA
PUBLISHER:
CONDÉ NAST S.P.A.
ART DIRECTOR:
ALBERTO NODOLINO
■ 4–6

PHOTOGRAPHER:
STEVEN KLEIN
CLIENT:
VOGUE PARIS
PUBLISHER:
CONDÉ NAST SA
ART DIRECTOR:
PAUL WAGNER
►■ 7

■ 4–6 "Colors: a Divertimento on the Theme of Black." The article appeared in the Italian edition of *Vogue.* (ITA)

■ 7 For an article on fashion in the Paris *Vogue:* "The Big Game". The model is designed by Gianfranco Ferré. (FRA)

■ 4–6 «Farben: Ein Zwischenspiel in Schwarz» – aus einem Modebeitrag in der italienischen *Vogue.* (ITA)

■ 7 Für einen Modebeitrag in *Vogue* Paris «Das grosse Spiel». Das gezeigte Modell ist von Gianfranco Ferré. (FRA)

■ 4–6 «Couleurs: divertissement en noir» – extrait d'un article de mode publié dans *Vogue* Italia. (ITA)

■ 7 Pour un article de mode de *Vogue* Paris intitulé «Le grand jeu». Le modèle est par Gianfranco Ferré. (FRA)

PHOTOGRAPHER:
Deborah Turbeville
CLIENT:
Loretta Di Lorenzo
DESIGNER:
Loretta Di Lorenzo
STUDIO:
Filomeno
■ 8, 9

PHOTOGRAPHER:
Javier Vallhonrat
CLIENT:
Vogue Italia
PUBLISHER:
Condé Nast S.p.A.
ART DIRECTOR:
Armando Nodolini
► ■ 10

■ 8, 9 Double-spread photographs from an advertising campaign for fashion by Loretta di Lorenzo as published in the Italian edition of *Vogue*. (ITA)

■ 10 Photograph from an article on draped clothing which appeared in the Italian edition of *Vogue*. (ITA)

■ 8, 9 Aus einer Kampagne mit doppelseitigen Aufnahmen für Mode von Loretta di Lorenzo, die in der italienischen *Vogue* erschien. (ITA)

■ 10 Aufnahme aus einem Modebeitrag in der italienischen *Vogue* über drapierte Kleider. (ITA)

■ 8, 9 Photos double page choisies parmi celles qui illustrent les modes Loretta di Lorenzo dans l'édition italienne du magazine *Vogue*. (ITA)

■ 10 Photo illustrant un article de mode de *Vogue* Italie consacré aux robes drapées. (ITA)

PHOTOGRAPHER:
MINSEI TOMINAGA
PUBLISHER:
COMME DES GARÇONS CO. LTD.
ART DIRECTOR:
TSUGUYA INOUE
◀ ■ 11

PHOTOGRAPHER:
RAFAEL BETZLER
CLIENT:
*AMADEUS FASHION
GESELLSCHAFT mbH*
ART DIRECTOR:
GERHARD PLAKOLM
DESIGNER:
GABI WAGNER
AGENCY:
DEMNER & MERLICEK
■ 12, 12a

■ 11 Photograph from a large-sized catalog featuring the 1988 fall and winter collection of Comme des Garçons. (JPN)

■ 12, 12a Full-page photographs from a catalog for *Amadeus Fashion* from Austria. (AUT)

■ 11 Aufnahme aus einem grossformatigen Katalog mit der Herbst-Winter-Kollektion '88 von Comme des Garçons. (JPN)

■ 12, 12a Ganzseitige Aufnahmen aus einem Katalog für *Amadeus Fashion,* Mode aus Österreich. (AUT)

■ 11 D'un catalogue au grand format présentant la collection automne/hiver 1988 de Comme des Garçons. (JPN)

■ 12, 12a Photos pleine page tirées d'un catalogue pour les modes autrichiennes *Amadeus Fashion.* (AUT)

PHOTOGRAPHER:
DEBORAH TURBEVILLE
CLIENT:
EMANUEL UNGARO
STUDIO:
FILOMENO
■ 13

■ 13 For a double-spread advertisement for evening wear by the fashion designer Emanuel Ungaro. (FRA)

■ 14 "Bathrooms in Antiquity: Aquatic Delight." The article was published in both the Italian and German editions of *Vogue*. (ITA/GER)

■ 13 Für eine doppelseitige Anzeige für Abendkleider des Modeschöpfers Emanuel Ungaro. (FRA)

■ 14 «Badezimmer der Antike: Die Wonnen im Wasser» ist der Titel dieses Beitrages in der deutschen *Vogue*, der ebenfalls in der italienischen Ausgabe erschienen ist. (ITA/GER)

■ 13 Pour une annonce double page pour les robes du soir du grand couturier Emanuel Ungaro. (FRA)

■ 14 «Salles de bains de l'Antiquité: la volupté au bain», tel est le titre de cet article paru à la fois dans l'édition allemande et dans l'édition italienne de *Vogue*. (ITA/GER)

PHOTOGRAPHER:
Deborah Turbeville
CLIENT:
Vogue Italia
Deutsche Vogue
PUBLISHER:
Condé Nast S.p.A.
Condé Nast Verlag GmbH
ART DIRECTOR:
Armando Nodolini
Angelica Blechschmidt
■ 14

PHOTOGRAPHER:
JOYCE TENNESON
PUBLISHER:
CONDÉ NAST PUBLICATIONS
ART DIRECTOR:
PHYLLIS COX
DESIGNER:
BETTY SARONSON
STUDIO:
BRIDE'S MAGAZINE
■ 15, 16

PHOTOGRAPHER:
Sheila Metzner
CLIENT:
Deutsche Vogue
PUBLISHER:
Condé Nast Verlag GmbH
ART DIRECTOR:
Angelica Blechschmidt
■ 17

■ 15, 16 Examples from an article on fashion entitled "Understatements" published in the American magazine *Bride's. 15* shows a petticoat from Christine and Co., and *16* shows a nightshirt by Calvin Klein. (USA)

■ 17 Evening dress by *Saint Laurent Rive Gauche* for the introductory double spread of an article entitled "Summer Stars" which appeared in the German *Vogue*. (GER)

■ 15, 16 Beispiele aus einem Modebeitrag mit dem Titel «Understatements» in der amerikanischen Zeitschrift *Bride's. 15* zeigt einen Petticoat von Christine and Co., *16* ein Nachthemd von Calvin Klein. (USA)

■ 17 Ein Abendkleid der Marke *Saint Laurent Rive Gauche* für die einleitende Doppelseite eines Beitrages unter dem Titel «Sommer-Stars» in der deutschen *Vogue*. (GER)

■ 15, 16 Exemples d'illustrations pour un article de mode paru sous le titre de «Understatements» dans le magazine américain *Bride's*. Fig. *15:* jupon de Christine and Co., fig. *16:* chemise de nuit de Calvin Klein. (USA)

■ 17 Robe du soir *Saint-Laurent Rive Gauche* sur la double page initiale d'un article de l'édition allemande de *Vogue* intitulé «Vedettes de l'été». (GER)

■ 18 Photograph from the fall/winter catalog 1987/88 for fashions of the *Complice* brand. (ITA)

■ 19 Photograph used by the Hornick/Rivlin Studio to promote its own work. (USA)

■ 20 Fashion photography by the American photographer Steve Hathaway for his own promotion. (USA)

■ 21 For an article in the German edition of *Vogue* entitled "Quintessence for your Beauty". (GER)

■ 18 Aufnahme aus einem Katalog für die Herbst/Winter-Kollektion 1987/88 für Mode der Marke *Complice*. (ITA)

■ 19 Für Eigenwerbung des Studios Hornick/Rivlin verwendete Modeaufnahme. (USA)

■ 20 Für Eigenwerbungszwecke verwendete Aufnahme des amerikanischen Photographen Steve Hathaway. (USA)

■ 21 Aus einem Beitrag in der deutschen *Vogue* mit dem Titel «Quintessenz für Ihre Schönheit». (GER)

■ 18 Photo tirée d'un catalogue pour la collection *Complice* de l'automne/hiver 1987/88. (ITA)

■ 19 Photo de mode que le studio Hornick/Rivlin, qui l'a réalisée, utilise pour ses besoins promotionnels. (USA)

■ 20 Photo de mode du photographe américain Steve Hathaway, utilisée pour la promotion de cet artiste. (USA)

■ 21 Photo pour un article de *Vogue* Allemagne intitulé «Quintessence de votre beauté». (GER)

PHOTOGRAPHER:
Marc Hispard
Art Director:
Nando Miglio
Agency:
Nando Miglio S.R.L.
Client:
Genny Moda S.P.A.
■ 18

PHOTOGRAPHER:
Rick Hornick
Stylist:
Keith Pollack
Client:
Potpourri Designs
Art Director:
Elaine Dalzell
Designer:
Studio John Clark
Studio:
Hornick/Rivlin
■ 19

PHOTOGRAPHER:
Steve Hathaway
■ 20

PHOTOGRAPHER:
Tyen
CLIENT:
Deutsche Vogue
PUBLISHER:
Condé Nast Verlag GmbH
ART DIRECTOR:
Angelica Blechschmidt
■ 21

PHOTOGRAPHER:
ALDO FALLAI
CLIENT:
L'UOMO
PUBLISHER:
CONDÉ NAST S.P.A.
DESIGNER:
PINO CHIARI
■ 22

■ 22 Photograph taken in Africa for an article in *L'Uomo*, the Italian magazine devoted to men's fashion. (ITA)

■ 23 Advertisement for fashion by Ralph Lauren. (USA)

■ 24 Sailor's bride from Föhr Island in her costume, from an article on this subject published in the *Frankfurter Allgemeine Magazin.* (GER)

■ 22 In Afrika entstandene Aufnahme für einen Modebeitrag im italienischen Herrenmodemagazin *L'Uomo.* (ITA)

■ 23 Anzeige für Mode von Ralph Lauren. (USA)

■ 24 Seemannsbraut mit Kopfputz – Porträt einer Föhringerin aus einem Beitrag über Trachten im *Frankfurter Allgemeine Magazin.* (GER)

■ 22 Photo réalisée en Afrique pour un article de mode du magazine italien de modes masculines *L'Uomo.* (ITA)

■ 23 Annonce pour les modes Ralph Lauren. (USA)

■ 24 Costume avec coiffe typique des fiancées de marins dans l'île de Föhr. Pour un article paru dans le *Frankfurter Allgemeine Magazin.* (GER)

PHOTOGRAPHER:
BRUCE WEBER
CLIENT:
RALPH LAUREN
ART DIRECTOR:
DONALD STERZIN
DESIGNER:
RALPH LAUREN
AGENCY:
WELLS, RICH, GREENE, INC.
■ 23

PHOTOGRAPHER:
SUSAN LAMER
PUBLISHER:
*FRANKFURTER ALLGEMEINE
ZEITUNG GMBH*
ART DIRECTOR:
HANS-GEORG POSPISCHIL
■ 24

PHOTOGRAPHER:
David Seidner
CLIENT:
Deutsche Vogue
PUBLISHER:
Condé Nast Verlag GmbH
ART DIRECTOR:
Angelica Blechschmidt
◄■ 25

PHOTOGRAPHER:
Frank Horvat
PUBLISHER:
Frankfurter Allgemeine Zeitung GmbH
ART DIRECTOR:
Hans-Georg Pospischil
■ 26, 27

■ 25 The comeback of the twin sets as featured in an article entitled "Twofold Wool Delight" in the German *Vogue*. (GER)

■ 26, 27 From an article on children published in the *Frankfurter Allgemeine Magazin*. (GER)

■ 25 Das Comeback der Twinsets ist das Thema eines Modebeitrags in der deutschen *Vogue* mit dem Titel «Woll-Lust mal zwei». (GER)

■ 26, 27 Aufnahmen aus einem Beitrag zum Thema Kinder im *Frankfurter Allgemeine Magazin*. (GER)

■ 25 Cet article de mode paru dans *Vogue* Allemagne traite du retour en force des twin-sets: «Volupté laineuse à double». (GER)

■ 26, 27 Photos illustrant un article sur les enfants paru dans le *Frankfurter Allgemeine Magazin*. (GER)

■ 28 Photograph from the promotional brochure of a hair salon in Toronto. (CAN)

■ 28 Aufnahme aus einem Werbeprospekt eines Coiffure-Salons in Toronto. (CAN)

■ 28 Photo illustrant le prospectus publicitaire d'un salon de coiffure à Toronto. (CAN)

■ 29 Double-spread ad for "Tea Rose" perfume. (USA)

■ 29 Doppelseitige Anzeige für das Parfum «Tea Rose». (USA)

■ 29 Annonce double page pour le parfum «Tea Rose». (USA)

PHOTOGRAPHER:
Deborah Samuel
STYLIST:
Loretta Chin
CLIENT:
Reinhart McMillan Hair Inc.
ART DIRECTOR:
Carmen Dunjko
DESIGNER:
Carmen Dunjko
AGENCY:
Carmen Dunjko Associates
◄■ 28

PHOTOGRAPHER:
John Chan
CLIENT:
The Perfumer's Workshop
ART DIRECTOR:
Isabella Gianameschi
DESIGNER:
John Chan
AGENCY:
*The Perfumer's Workshop/
In House*
■ 29

PHOTOGRAPHER:
MICHAEL ROBERTS
CLIENT:
VOGUE PARIS
PUBLISHER:
CONDÉ NAST SA
ART DIRECTOR:
PAUL WAGNER
■ 30, 31

■ 30, 31 Fashion photographs inspired by Jean Genet's novel *Notre-Dame-des-Fleurs*, and taken by the photographer and painter Michael Roberts for the French edition of *Vogue*. (FRA)

■ 32 From an article in the *Frankfurter Allgemeine Magazin* on the French fashion designer Christian Lacroix and entitled "Imagination's Cause for Celebration". (GER)

■ 30, 31 Inspiriert durch den Roman *Notre-Dame-des-Fleurs* von Jean Genet entstanden diese Modeaufnahmen des Photographen und Malers Michael Roberts für die französische Ausgabe von *Vogue*. (FRA)

■ 32 Aus einem Beitrag im *Frankfurter Allgemeine Magazin* über den französischen Modeschöpfer Christian Lacroix mit dem Titel «Die Phantasie feiert ein Fest». (GER)

■ 30, 31 Ces photos de mode du photographe et peintre Michael Roberts s'inspirent du roman contestataire de Jean Genet, *Notre-Dame-des-Fleurs*. Tirées de l'édition française de *Vogue*. (FRA)

■ 32 Pour un article du *Frankfurter Allgemeine Magazin* où il est question du grand couturier français Christian Lacroix. Le titre: «L'imagination en fête.» (GER)

PHOTOGRAPHER:
SARAH MOON
PUBLISHER:
FRANKFURTER ALLGMEINE
ZEITUNG GMBH
ART DIRECTOR:
HANS-GEORG POSPISCHIL
■ 32

PHOTOGRAPHER:
SNOWDON
CLIENT:
L'UOMO
PUBLISHER:
CONDÉ NAST S.P.A.
DESIGNER:
PINO CHIARI
■ 33-35

■ 33–35 From an article entitled "Hamlet's Misgivings" published in the men's fashion magazine *L'Uomo*. It presents an interpretation by Snowdon of the choreographer and dancer Michael Clark's vocation to dandyism. (ITA)

■ 33–35 Die Berufung des Tänzers und Choreographen Michael Clark zum Dandy, interpretiert von Snowdon. Aus einem Modebeitrag mit dem Titel «Hamlets Zweifel» im italienischen Herrenmagazin *L'Uomo*. (ITA)

■ 33–35 La vocation de dandy du danseur-chorégraphe Michael Clark interprétée par l'objectif vigilant de Snowdon. Pour un article de mode intitulé «Les doutes de Hamlet», paru dans le magazine italien *L'Uomo*. (ITA)

PHOTOGRAPHER:
PETER LINDBERGH
PUBLISHER:
MARIE CLAIRE
ART DIRECTOR:
WALTER ROSPERT
■ 36, 37

■ 36, 37 Homage to the famous photographer Jacques-Henri Lartigue and to his model Renée Perle. From an article in the magazine *Marie Claire* with illustrations of fashion in the style of the 1930's. (FRA)

■ 38 From a campaign for American Express. (USA)

■ 36, 37 Hommage an den berühmten Photographen Jacques-Henri Lartigue und sein Modell Renée Perle. Aus einem Beitrag in der Zeitschrift *Marie Claire* mit Mode im Stil der dreissiger Jahre. (FRA)

■ 38 Aus einer Werbekampagne für American Express. (USA)

■ 36, 37 Hommage au célèbre photographe Jacques-Henri Lartigue et à son modèle Renée Perle. Article du magazine *Marie Claire* où il est question de la mode actuelle rappelant le style des années 30. (FRA)

■ 38 D'une campagne pour American Express. (USA)

PHOTOGRAPHER:
HANS NELEMAN
CLIENT:
AMERICAN EXPRESS
ART DIRECTOR:
ROB BOEZEWINKEL
AGENCY:
OGILVY & MATHER
■ 38

PHOTOGRAPHER:
GARY NOLTON
CLIENT:
NIKE, INC.
ART DIRECTOR:
STEVEN SANDSTROM
DESIGNER:
STEVEN SANDSTROM
AGENCY:
NIKE DESIGN
■ 39

■ 39 From an ad campaign for *Nike* sports shoes. (USA)

■ 40 Double-spread photograph from an article on fashion in the American edition of the magazine *Elle*. (USA)

■ 39 Aus einer Werbekampagne für *Nike*-Sportschuhe. (USA)

■ 40 Doppelseitige Aufnahme aus einem Modebeitrag in der amerikanischen Ausgabe der Zeitschrift *Elle*. (USA)

■ 39 Campagne pour les chaussures de sport *Nike*. (USA)

■ 40 Photo double page illustrant un article de mode paru dans l'édition américaine du magazine *Elle*. (USA)

PHOTOGRAPHER:
Gilles Bensimon
PUBLISHER:
Elle Magazine
ART DIRECTOR:
Phyllis Schefer
■ 40

PHOTOGRAPHER:
Nicoletta Giordano
CLIENT:
L'Uomo
PUBLISHER:
Condé Nast S.p.A.
DESIGNER:
Pino Chiari
■ 41, 42

PHOTOGRAPHER:
Bill White
STYLIST:
Bill White
ART DIRECTOR:
Bill White
► ■ 43

■ 41, 42 "Cottonwear" is the title of this article on fashion which appeared in the magazine *L'Uomo*. (ITA)

■ 43 Photograph by the New York photographer Bill White for his own promotion. (USA)

■ 41, 42 «Cottonwear» ist der Titel dieses Modebeitrags in der Zeitschrift *L'Uomo*. (ITA)

■ 43 Aufnahme für Eigenwerbungszwecke des New Yorker Photographen Bill White. (USA)

■ 41, 42 Cet article de mode est publié par le magazine *L'Uomo* sous le titre de «Cottonwear». (ITA)

■ 43 Photo réalisée par le photographe new-yorkais Bill White pour les besoins de sa promotion. (USA)

PHOTOGRAPHER:
IVO V. RENNER
CLIENT:
MEDIMA
AGENCY:
LINTAS HAMBURG
■ 44

PHOTOGRAPHER:
ALAXANDAR JOSEPHS
ART DIRECTOR:
ALAXANDAR JOSEPHS
DESIGNER:
ALAXANDAR JOSEPHS
STUDIO:
ALAXANDAR PHOTOGRAPHY
► ■ 45–48

■ 44 Photograph from an advertising brochure by Medima, a manufacturer of men's and women's underclothing. (GER)

■ 45–48 Examples from a loose-leaf brochure sent by the Alaxandar photography studio to health clubs and spas for the promotion of its own work. (USA)

■ 44 Aufnahme aus einem Werbeprospekt der Firma Medima, Hersteller von Damen- und Herrenwäsche. (GER)

■ 45–48 Beispiele aus einem Prospekt mit losen Blättern, den das Photostudio Alaxandar als Eigenwerbung an Fitness-Clubs und Heilbäder verschickt. (USA)

■ 44 Photo pour un prospectus publicitaire de la maison Medima, fabricant de sous-vêtements et lingerie. (GER)

■ 45–48 Photos illustrant un prospectus à feuilles mobiles que le studio de photographie Alaxandar fait parvenir aux clubs de fitness et aux stations thermales. (USA)

■ 53 Coat and tie serve as a symbol of the businessman. This photograph was used by Eurocard in the Netherlands for its own promotion. (NLD)

■ 54, 55 Gray is the newest trend for men's fashion in an article published by the magazine *L'Uomo*. (ITA)

■ 53 Hemd und Krawatte als Symbol für den Geschäftsmann. Diese Aufnahme wurde von Eurocard Nederland für ihre Werbung verwendet. (NLD)

■ 54, 55 Die neue Männermode in Grau ist das Thema dieses Beitrags in der Zeitschrift *L'Uomo*. (ITA)

■ 53 Chemise et cravate, les emblèmes de l'homme d'affaires. Cette photo a été utilisée par l'Eurocard néerlandaise pour sa publicité. (NLD)

■ 54, 55 La nouvelle mode masculine en gris tient la vedette de cet article paru dans le magazine *L'Uomo*. (ITA)

PHOTOGRAPHER:
FABRIZIO GIANNI
CLIENT:
L'UOMO
PUBLISHER:
CONDÉ NAST S.P.A.
DESIGNER:
PINO CHIARI
■ 54, 55

■ 56 "Farmers" is the title of this photograph taken by H. R. Feltus for Trotinette, Paris. (FRA)

■ 57 From an article in the Italian *Vogue* describing fashion in the styles of the 1920's, 30's, 40's and 50's. The example is from the collection of Salvatore Ferragamo. (ITA)

■ 56 «Farmers» ist der Titel dieser Aufnahme, die der Photograph H. R. Feltus for Trotinette, Paris, machte. (FRA)

■ 57 Für einen Beitrag in der italienischen *Vogue* über die Mode im Stile der 20er, 30er, 40er und 50er Jahre. Hier ein Beispiel aus der Kollektion von Salvatore Ferragamo. (ITA)

■ 56 Cette photo réalisée par le photographe H. R. Feltus pour Trotinette (Paris) est intitulée «Farmers». (FRA)

■ 57 Pour un article de *Vogue Italia* consacré à la mode évoquant les années 20, 30, 40 et 50. L'exemple présenté ici fait partie de la collection Salvatore Ferragamo. (ITA)

PHOTOGRAPHER:
H. Ross Feltus
CLIENT:
Trotinette
ART DIRECTOR:
H. Ross Feltus
DESIGNER:
H. Ross Feltus
◄ ■ 56

PHOTOGRAPHER:
David Ken
CLIENT:
Vogue Italia
PUBLISHER:
Condé Nast S.p.A.
ART DIRECTOR:
Armando Nodolini
■ 57

PHOTOGRAPHER:
Marianne Chemetov
STYLIST:
Brana Wolf
CLIENT:
Vogue Paris
PUBLISHER:
Condé Nast SA
ART DIRECTOR:
Paul Wagner
■ 58

PHOTOGRAPHER:
ANDRÉA BLANCH
STYLIST:
MADELEINE COFANO (HAIR)/
LAURA MERCIER (MAKE-UP)
CLIENT:
MICHÈLLE MARC
ART DIRECTOR:
MARC BENHAMOU
AGENCY:
VOGUE PROMOTION
■ 59

PHOTOGRAPHER:
STAN MALINOWSKI
PUBLISHER:
METRO PUBLISHING
ART DIRECTOR:
STAN MALINOWSKI
DESIGNER;
STAN MALINOWSKI
■ 60

■ 58 From an article in *Vogue.* Paris on the new make up colors, here by Yves Saint Laurent. The hat is by Philippe Model, the dress by Martine Sitbon. (FRA)

■ 59 Photograph for fashions by Michèlle Marc published in the advertising section of the American *Vogue.* (USA)

■ 60 Cover photograph from the first issue of *Metro,* a magazine dedicated to fashion and newsmakers. (USA)

■ 58 Aus einem Beitrag in *Vogue* Paris über die neuen Make-up-Farben, hier von Yves Saint Laurent. Der Hut ist von Philippe Model, das Kleid von Martine Sitbon. (FRA)

■ 59 Ganzseitige Aufnahme aus dem Promotionsteil der amerikanischen *Vogue* für Mode von Michèlle Marc. (USA)

■ 60 Umschlagphoto der ersten Ausgabe von *Metro,* einer Zeitschrift über Mode und Gesellschaft. (USA)

■ 58 D'un article de *Vogue* Paris sur les nouveux couleurs de maquillage, ici par Yves Saint Laurent. Chapeau par Philippe Model, robe par Martine Sitbon. (FRA)

■ 59 Photo pleine page illustrant les modes Michèlle Marc dans la section promotionnelle de *Vogue* Amérique. (USA)

■ 60 Photo de couverture du premier numéro de *Metro,* un magazine trimestriel de mode et de société. (USA)

PHOTOGRAPHER:
Robin Thompson
STYLIST:
Sheenia Gates
CLIENT:
Jaeger
ART DIRECTOR:
Jeremy Perrott
DESIGNER:
Jeremy Perrott
AGENCY:
Optimus Graphic Design Ltd.
■ 61

■ 61 Unpublished photograph for a planned campaign by Jaeger as promotion for their fashionable clothing. (GBR)

■ 61 Unveröffentlichte Aufnahme für eine geplante Werbekampagne des Modeherstellers Jaeger. (GBR)

■ 61 Photo inédite pour une promotion associée à un concours organisé par le grand couturier Jaeger. (GBR)

AUSSENAUFNAHMEN

PHOTOGRAPHER:
WALTER VETSCH 62
BEAT KÄSLIN 63
LARRY DALE GORDON/
THE IMAGE BANK 64
PUBLISHER:
SWISS AIR TRANSPORT
COMPANY LTD.
ART DIRECTOR:
EMIL SCHULTHESS/
FRITZ GIRARDIN
◄■ 62–64

PHOTOGRAPHER:
JOHN CLARIDGE
PUBLISHER:
GLIMPSELAND LIMITED
ART DIRECTOR:
CHRIS LOWER
DESIGNER:
DESIGN HOUSE CONSULTANTS
■ 65

■ 62–64 Photographs from the 1988 Swissair wall calendar. *62* shows several layers of altocumulus lenticularis above the 6997-meter Machapuchhare, often known as the "Matterhorn of Nepal"; *63:* lens-shaped foehn clouds over Central Switzerland; *64:* storm clouds over the state of Wyoming, USA. (SWI)

■ 65 "Clouds and Sea", Wales 1987. Photograph from the book *One Hundred Photographs* by John Claridge. (GBR)

■ 62–64 Aufnahmen aus dem Swissair-Kalender 1988. *62:* eine in mehreren Schichten angeordnete Altocumulus-lenticularis-Wolke über dem Machapuchhare (6997 m), dem «Matterhorn Nepals»; *63:* linsenförmige Föhnwolken über den Innerschweizer Alpen; *64:* Gewitterwolken über Wyoming, USA. (SWI)

■ 65 «Wolken und Meer», Wales 1987. Aufnahme aus dem Buch *One Hundred Photographs* von John Claridge. (GBR)

■ 62–64 Photos du calendrier Swissair pour 1988. *62:* dans l'onde ascendante du Machapuchhare (6997 m), le «Cervin du Népal», s'est formée cette lentille géante à plusieurs étages; *63:* nuages de fœhn lenticulaires au-dessus des Alpes de Suisse centrale; *64:* cumulo-nimbus annonçant un orage au-dessus du Wyoming aux Etats-Unis. (SWI)

■ 65 «Nuages et mer», pays de Galles 1987. Photo illustrant le livre *One Hundred Photographs* de John Claridge. (GBR)

PHOTOGRAPHER:
NEIL LUKAS
CLIENT:
NEIL LUKAS
◄ ■ 66

PHOTOGRAPHER:
KAREN MALOOF
PUBLISHER:
CATCH PUBLISHING
■ 67

■ 66 "Café Diderot", shot by London photographer Neil Lukas and used by him as self-promotion. (GBR)

■ 67 "Skytop", photograph taken by Karen Maloof and available on general sale to the public. (NLD)

■ 66 «Café Diderot», als Eigenwerbung verwendete Aufnahme des Londoner Photographen Neil Lukas. (GBR)

■ 67 Eine im Handel erhältliche Aufnahme («Skytop») der Photographin Karen Maloof. (NLD)

■ 66 «Café Diderot», photo du photographe londonien Neil Lukas que celui-ci utilise pour son autopromotion. (GBR)

■ 67 Photo «Skytop» de la photographe Karen Maloof commercialisée aux Pays-Bas. (NLD)

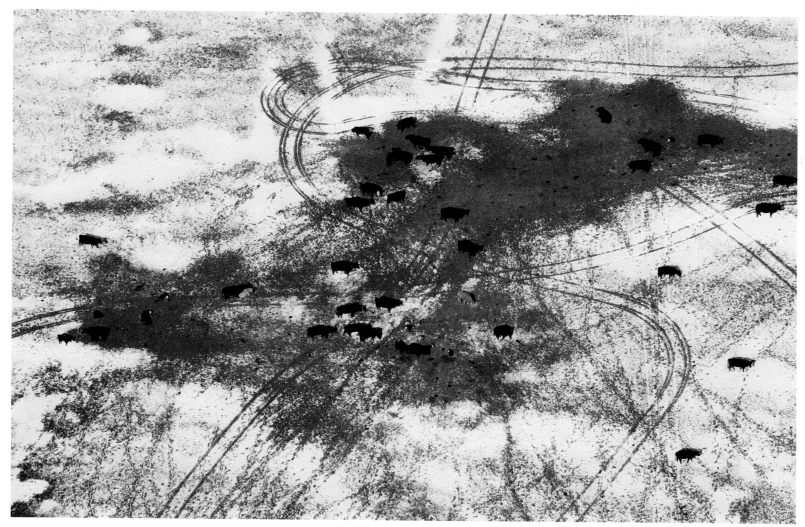

PHOTOGRAPHER:
DAVID KRAMER
CLIENT:
INK SPOT
ART DIRECTOR:
MARK WRONSKI
DESIGNER:
MARK WRONSKI
AGENCY:
JANSEN & ASSOCIATES
◄■ 68

PHOTOGRAPHER:
ROBERT LLEWELLYN
CLIENT:
MEAD PAPER
ART DIRECTOR:
ROBERT FRANKLE
DESIGNER:
ROBERT FRANKLE
AGENCY:
COOK & SHANOSKY
■ 69

■ 68 Photograph from a calendar for Ink Spot. (USA)

■ 69 "Snow-sugared prairie like a vast gingerbread, raisined with feeding cattle". Photograph taken from a brochure for *Mead* paper. (USA)

■ 68 Aufnahme aus einem Kalender für Ink Spot. (USA)

■ 69 Wie Puderzucker liegt der Schnee auf der Prairie; die weidenden Rinder wirken wie Rosinen. Aufnahme aus einer Broschüre für *Mead*-Papier. (USA)

■ 68 Photo illustrant un calendrier d'Ink Spot. (USA)

■ 69 La neige saupoudrant la prairie évoque un pain d'épice où le bétail représenterait les raisins secs. Photo tirée d'une brochure des papiers *Mead*. (USA)

■ 70-73 From an article about Brittany appearing in the Dutch magazine *Avenue:* a 19th century castle *(70);* on All Saints' Day (1st November) in Plougastel Daoulas, a mass is held for the dead and their graves are decorated *(71, 72);* the Celts offered sacrifices to one of their gods under this cross *(73).* (NLD)

■ 70-73 Aus einem Beitrag über die Bretagne in *Avenue:* Ein Schloss aus dem 19. Jahrhundert *(70);* am 1. November (Allerheiligen) wird in Plougastel Daoulas auf dem Friedhof eine Messe für die Toten gehalten und die Gräber werden geschmückt *(71, 72);* unter diesem Kreuz opferten die Kelten einem ihrer Götter *(73).* (NLD)

■ 70-73 Pour un article que le magazine hollandais *Avenue* consacre à la Bretagne: château du XIXe siècle *(70);* à la Toussaint, le 1er novembre, une messe de requiem est célébrée au cimetière de Plougastel Daoulas dont les tombes sont décorées *(71, 72);* c'est sous cette croix que les Gaulois rendaient jadis un culte à l'un de leurs dieux *(73).* (NLD)

PHOTOGRAPHER:
MARTIN KERS
PUBLISHER:
DE GEILLUSTREERDE PERS B.V.
ART DIRECTOR:
HANS VAN BLOMMESTEIN
■ 70-73

PHOTOGRAPHER:
STEPHAN ERFURT
PUBLISHER:
*FRANKFURTER ALLGEMEINE
ZEITUNG GMBH*
ART DIRECTOR:
HANS-GEORG POSPISCHIL
◄■ 74, 75

PHOTOGRAPHER:
ALBERT WATSON
CLIENT:
BLUMARINE
ART DIRECTOR:
MANUELA PAVESI
DESIGNER:
SMATT FLORENCE
AGENCY:
MODENESE & MODENESE
■ 76

■ 74, 75 Photographs from an article in the *Frankfurter Allgemeine Magazin* about the liner "Queen Mary" that is permanently anchored at the pier of Long Beach, California, and has become a popular tourist attraction. (GER)

■ 76 A Scottish railway bridge on the cover of an ad insert in *Vogue Italia* with fashions by Blumarine. (ITA)

■ 74, 75 Aufnahmen aus einem Beitrag im *Frankfurter Allgemeine Magazin* über die «Queen Mary», die am Pier von Long Beach, Kalifornien, für immer festliegt und zu einer Touristen-Attraktion geworden ist. (GER)

■ 76 Eine Eisenbahnbrücke in Schottland für den Umschlag einer Werbebeilage mit Mode von Blumarine. (ITA)

■ 74, 75 Photos illustrant un article du *Frankfurter Allgemeine Magazin* sur le «Queen Mary» immobilisé à tout jamais à Long Beach, en Californie, où le fier paquebot sert d'attraction pour les touristes. (GER)

■ 76 Pont de chemin de fer écossais sur la couverture d'un encart publicitaire des modes Blumarine. (ITA)

■ 77 From a series of photographs by Matt Mahurin published in *Regardie's* magazine under the theme of "Visions of Stone" – together with texts relating to human destiny contributed by various authors. (USA)

■ 78 For the cover of a calendar for Stephenson Inc. of Alexandria, Virginia. (USA)

■ 77 Aus einer Reihe von Aufnahmen von Matt Mahurin, die unter dem Thema «Visionen von Stein» zusammen mit Texten verschiedener Schriftsteller über das menschliche Schicksal in *Regardie's* veröffentlicht wurden. (USA)

■ 78 Für die Vorderseite eines Kalenders der Stephenson Inc. aus Alexandria, Virginia. (USA)

■ 77 Exemple des photos prises par Matt Mahurin sous le titre générique de «Visions de pierre». Elles accompagnent des textes d'écrivains sur le thème du destin de l'homme. Magazine *Regardie's*. (USA)

■ 78 Pour le feuillet de couverture d'un calendrier de la Stephenson Inc. d'Alexandria, en Virginie. (USA)

PHOTOGRAPHER:
MATT MAHURIN
PUBLISHER:
REGARDIE'S
ART DIRECTOR:
FRED WOODWARD
DESIGNER:
FRED WOODWARD
◀ ■ 77

PHOTOGRAPHER:
LARRY OLSEN
CLIENT:
STEPHENSON, INC.
DESIGNER:
JOHN MICHAEL
■ 78

PHOTOGRAPHER:
HARRY DE ZITTER
CLIENT:
DE ZITTER PHOTOGRAPHY
ART DIRECTOR:
HARRY DE ZITTER
STUDIO:
HARRY DE ZITTER
■ 79–82

■ 79–82 Photographs used as self-promotion by Harry De Zitter. (GBR)

■ 79–82 Als Eigenwerbung des Photographen Harry De Zitter verwendete Aufnahmen. (GBR)

■ 79–82 Photos autopromotionnelles du photographe Harry De Zitter. (GBR)

PHOTOGRAPHER:
Harry De Zitter

CLIENT:
De Zitter Photography

ART DIRECTOR:
Harry De Zitter

STUDIO:
Harry De Zitter

■ 83-85

PHOTOGRAPHER:
HARRY DE ZITTER
CLIENT:
ICI
ART DIRECTOR:
MATT RIAN
AGENCY:
SAATCHI & SAATCHI
■ 86

■ 83–85 Impressions of America by photographer Harry De Zitter, used by him as self-promotion. (GBR)

■ 86 For a corporate image campaign of ICI. (GBR)

■ 83–85 Amerikanische Impressionen des Photographen Harry De Zitter, die er als Eigenwerbung verwendet. (GBR)

■ 86 Für eine Corporate-Image-Kampagne von ICI. (GBR)

■ 83–85 Impressions d'Amérique réalisées par le photographe Harry De Zitter et utilisées pour sa promotion. (GBR)

■ 86 Pour une campagne d'image globale d'ICI. (GBR)

PHOTOGRAPHER:
KAREN MALOOF
PUBLISHER:
CATCH PUBLISHING
■ 87

■ 87 "Boat on Sea", photograph by Karen Maloof on general sale. (NLD)

■ 88 "Citroën", shot for a self-promotional poster taken by photographer Nadav Kander. (GBR)

■ 89 Self-promotion by London photographer Pete Seaward. (GBR)

■ 87 Eine im Handel erhältliche Aufnahme («Boat on Sea») von Karen Maloof. (NLD)

■ 88 «Citroën», für ein Eigenwerbungsplakat verwendete Aufnahme des Photographen Nadav Kander. (GBR)

■ 89 Eigenwerbung des Londoner Photographen Pete Seaward. (GBR)

■ 87 Photo («Boat on Sea») de Karen Maloof entrée dans le circuit commercial. (NLD)

■ 88 «Citroën», photo du photographe Nadav Kander, qui l'utilise pour sa publicité par voie d'affiche. (GBR)

■ 89 Autopromotion du photographe londonien Pete Seaward. (GBR)

Photographer:
Nadav Kander
Client:
Nadav Kander Photography
Art Director:
Trevor Kennedy
Designer:
Nadav Kander/John Gorham
▼■ 88

Photographer:
▼ *Pete Seaward*
▼■ 89

PHOTOGRAPHER:
RICHARD MISRACH
PUBLISHER:
*FRANKFURTER ALLGEMEINE
ZEITUNG GMBH*
ART DIRECTOR:
HANS-GEORG POSPISCHIL
■ 90, 91

■ 90, 91 Photographs from an article in the *Frankfurter All-gemeine Magazin* entitled "Myths of Sand and Stone: The Desert". Richard Misrach took the shots in Southern California. He shows a desert whose temporary inhabitants have left their traces. (GER)

■ 90, 91 Aufnahmen aus einem Artikel im *Frankfurter All-gemeine Magazin* mit dem Titel «Mythos aus Sand und Stein: Die Wüste». Richard Misrach photographierte im süd-lichen Kalifornien; er zeigt eine Wüste, die vom Menschen gezeichnet ist. (GER)

■ 90, 91 Photos tirées d'un article du *Frankfurter Allge-meine Magazin* intitulé «Mythe de sable et de pierres: le désert». Richard Misrach les a réalisées dans le sud de la Californie. Il montre un désert que l'homme a marqué de sa griffe. (GER)

PHOTOGRAPHER:
STEPHEN WILKES
PUBLISHER:
FRIENDLY PRESS, INC.
DESIGNER:
MARTY GOLDSTEIN
■ 92-96

■ 92-96 Photographs taken from a book issued by the Friendly Press entitled *California One: The Pacific Coast Highway,* a photographic essay about this highway that runs from Leggett in North California to Dana Point in the South. (USA)

■ 92-96 Aufnahmen aus einem bei Friendly Press erschienenen Buch mit dem Titel *California One: The Pacific Coast Highway,* ein photographischer Bericht über diese Strasse, die von Leggett im Norden Kaliforniens nach Dana Point im Süden führt. (USA)

■ 92-96 Photos extraites d'un ouvrage paru aux Ed. Friendly Press, *California One: The Pacific Coast Highway,* reportage photo sur cette artère côtière qui mène de Leggett au nord jusqu'à Dana Point au sud le long du Pacifique. (USA)

PHOTOGRAPHER:
SCOTT BARROW
PUBLISHER:
FOREMOST PUBLISHERS, INC.
DESIGNER:
DONALD G. PAULHUS
■ 97

■ 97 From one of the photo books published by Foremost Publishers, Inc. entitled *Extraordinary New Jersey.* Shown is a shot of "Seaside Park" on the New Jersey coast. (USA)

■ 97 Aus einem bei Foremost Publishers, Inc. erschienenen Photoband mit dem Titel *Extraordinary New Jersey.* Hier der «Seaside Park» an der Küste New Jerseys. (USA)

■ 97 Pour un album photo paru aux Editions Foremost Publishers, Inc. sous le titre de *Extraordinary New Jersey.* On voit ici le «Seaside Park» sur la côte du New Jersey. (USA)

PHOTOGRAPHER:
Ken Straiton
PUBLISHER:
Minolta Camera Co. Ltd.
ART DIRECTOR:
Fred O. Bechlen
■ 98

■98 University building in art déco style in Montreal on a winter afternoon. The vapor clouds engender an almost extraterrestrial atmosphere. From the magazine *Minolta Mirror.* (JPN)

■99 Photograph for Leisure Technology, a senior citizens' housing development. (USA)

■98 Universitätsgebäude im Art-Déco-Stil in Montreal an einem Nachmittag im Winter. Die Dampfwolken erzeugen eine fast ausserirdische Atmosphäre. Aus der Zeitschrift *Minolta Mirror.* (JPN)

■99 Aufnahme für Leisure Technology, ein Bauunternehmen für Alterswohnungen. (USA)

■98 Bâtiment universitaire de style Art nouveau à Montréal, par un après-midi d'hiver. Les nuages de vapeur créent une ambiance quasi extraterrestre. Tiré du *Minolta Mirror.* (JPN)

■99 Photo pour Leisure Technology, entreprise qui construit des logements pour le 3e âge. (USA)

PHOTOGRAPHER:
Lonnie Duka
CLIENT:
Leisure Technology
ART DIRECTOR:
Gary Hinsche
DESIGNER:
Gary Hinsche
AGENCY:
Robert Miles
Runyan & Associates
■ 99

■ 100–103 From a new book published by Prentice Hall, entitled *Manhattan Architecture. 100:* A picture of the contrasts in New York's financial district – in the foreground a building at No. 90 West Street, and the World Trade Center. *101:* The inner court of the Alwyn Court apartment house with a trompe l'œil mural by Richard Haas; *102:* Atlas (with clock) at Tiffany's at No. 727 Fifth Avenue (crafted by Harry Frederick Metzler, 1853). *103:* A section of the Chrysler Building. (USA)

■ 100–103 Aus einem bei Prentice Hall erschienenen Bildband: *Manhattan Architecture. 100:* Ein Bild des Kontrastes in New Yorks Finanzdistrikt – ein Gebäude an der West Street No. 90 im Vordergrund und das World Trade Center. *101:* Der Lichthof des Alwyn Court Apartment-Hauses mit Trompe-L'Œil-Wandmalerei von Richard Haas; *102:* Atlas (mit Uhr) bei Tiffany's an der Fifth Avenue Nr. 727 (von Harry Frederick Metzler, 1853). *103:* Detail des Chrysler-Gebäudes. (USA)

■ 100–103 Pour un album publié chez Prentice Hall sous le titre *Manhattan Architecture. 100:* Dans le district financier, contraste étonnant entre cette maison de West Street 90 et le World Trade Center. *101:* La cour d'aération du locatif d'Alwyn Court décorée d'un mural de Richard Haas peint en trompe-l'œil d'après la décoration originale de 1909. *102:* Atlas portant l'horloge chez Tiffany's au 727 de Fifth Avenue, une création de Harry Frederick Metzler en 1853. *103:* Détail du Building Chrysler. (USA)

PHOTOGRAPHER:
RICHARD BERENHOLTZ
PUBLISHER:
PRENTICE HALL PRESS
ART DIRECTOR:
JEAN-CLAUDE SUARES
DESIGNER:
SUZANNE REISEL/
JEAN-CLAUDE SUARES
AGENCY:
PRENTICE HALL PRESS
■ 100–103

PHOTOGRAPHER:
NIKOLAY ZUREK
CLIENT:
PACIFIC GAS + ELECTRIC CO.
DESIGNER:
NEIL SHAKERY
AGENCY:
PENTAGRAM
■ 104

PHOTOGRAPHER:
KAREN I. HIRSCH
■ 105

■ 104 Photograph used in an annual report for the Pacific Gas + Electric Co. (USA)

■ 105 View of the Marina City Building in Chicago. (USA)

■ 106–109 Ranchos de Taos Church, New Mexico – a popular tourist attraction and subject for photographers and artists. In his shots Doug Keats concentrates on the play of light. Shown are examples from the series that appeared in the French magazine *Zoom.* (FRA)

■ 104 Für einen Jahresbericht der Pacific Gas + Electric Co. verwendete Aufnahme. (USA)

■ 105 Ansicht des Marina City Buildings in Chicago. (USA)

■ 106–109 Die Kirche von Ranchos de Taos in Neumexiko, Touristenattraktion und beliebtes Thema für Photographen und Maler. Doug Keats konzentrierte sich bei seinen Aufnahmen auf das Spiel des Lichtes. Hier einige Beispiele aus der Serie, die in *Zoom* veröffentlicht wurden. (FRA)

■ 104 Photo utilisée pour l'illustration d'un rapport annuel de la Pacific Gas + Electric Co. (USA)

■ 105 Vue du Marina City building à Chicago. (USA)

■ 106–109 L'église de Rancho de Taos au Nouveau-Mexique, attraction touristique en même temps qu'un sujet de prédilection pour peintres et photographes. Dans ses photos, Doug Keats insiste sur les jeux de lumière. On trouve ici quelques exemples de la série publiée dans *Zoom.* (FRA)

PHOTOGRAPHER:
Doug Keats
PUBLISHER:
Zoom
ART DIRECTOR:
Joel Laroche
■ 106–109

PHOTOGRAPHER:
MARK SEGAL
CLIENT:
CITICORP
ART DIRECTOR:
BOB GALLANO
DESIGNER:
TERRY DALE
◀■ 112–114

PHOTOGRAPHER:
ROBERT LAUTMAN
PUBLISHER:
CONDÉ NAST PUBLICATIONS INC.
ART DIRECTOR:
KAREN LEE GRANT
DESIGNER:
KAREN LEE GRANT
■ 115

■ 112–114 Examples of the panoramic photos from the 1988 calendar for Citicorp. The subject is Washington and all shots were taken by Mark Segal. He used a specially built panoramic camera that can rotate in a circle and expose up to a full 360° panorama on a flat piece of film. Shown is the Jefferson Memorial *(112, 113)* and a view from the Lincoln Memorial towards the east. (USA)

■ 115 Night view of the swimming pool of a Caribbean-style house designed by architect Hugh Newell Jacobsen. From an article in the magazine *House & Garden*. (USA)

■ 112–114 Aus einem Kalender für Citicorp. Das Thema ist Washington, und alle Aufnahmen wurden von Mark Segal mit einer speziell konstruierten Panorama-Kamera gemacht. Mit ihr lässt sich ein Panorama von bis zu 360° auf ein flaches Stück Film bringen. Hier das Jefferson Memorial *(112, 113)* und ein Blick vom Lincoln Memorial gen Osten. (USA)

■ 115 Blick auf den nächtlichen Swimming-Pool eines Hauses des Architekten Hugh Newell Jacobsen im karibischen Stil. Aus der Zeitschrift *House & Garden*. (USA)

■ 112–114 Photos illustrant un calendrier de Citicorp. Le thème choisi est la ville de Washington. Tous les clichés ont été réalisés par Mark Segal à l'aide d'une caméra panoramique de sa construction, qui permet de faire entrer une vue à 360° dans une pellicule rectangulaire. On voit ici le Jefferson Memorial *(112, 113)* et une vue depuis le Lincoln Memorial. (USA)

■ 115 Vue nocturne de la piscine d'une maison que l'architecte Hugh Newell Jacobsen a construite dans le style des Caraïbes. Photo tirée du magazine *House & Garden*. (USA)

PHOTOGRAPHER:
JAIME MALÉ
CLIENT:
MUEBLES LA FAVORITA
ART DIRECTOR:
EDUARDO MALÉ
DESIGNER:
MIGUEL GARIGLIANO
AGENCY:
CONCEPTUAL
■ 116, 117

■ 116, 117 Photographs
for the Spanish furniture
producer Muebles la
Favorita. (SPA)

■ 116, 117 Für den spani-
schen Möbelhersteller
Muebles La Favorita entstandene Aufnahmen. (SPA)

■ 116, 117 Photos réalisées
pour le fabricant d'ameuble-
ments espagnol Muebles
La Favorita. (SPA)

PHOTOGRAPHER:
Frank Herholdt
CLIENT:
Amtico
ART DIRECTOR:
Kim Richmond
DESIGNER:
Kim Richmond
AGENCY:
Brooks and Vernons
■ 118, 119

■ 118, 119 "Works of art you can walk on" is the slogan for these shots used in a calendar and in advertisements for the carpet producers Amtico. (GBR)

■ 118, 119 «Kunstwerke, auf denen man gehen kann» ist der Slogan für diese Aufnahmen, die der Teppichhersteller Amtico in einem Kalender und in Anzeigen verwendet. (GBR)

■ 118, 119 «Des chefs-d'œuvre qu'on peut fouler aux pieds» – photos du fabricant de tapis Amtico utlisées pour un calendrier et une campagne d'annonces. (GBR)

PHOTOGRAPHER:
RJ Muna
■ 120

■ 120 Personal study by photographer R. J. Muna, Palo Alto. (USA)

■ 120 Persönliche Studie des Photographen R. J. Muna, Palo Alto. (USA)

■ 120 Etude personnelle du photographe R. J. Muna Palo Alto. (USA)

PHOTOGRAPHER:
PHILIP QUIRK
CLIENT:
WORLD EXPO 88 AUTHORITY,
BRISBANE
ART DIRECTOR:
KEN CATO
DESIGNER:
KEN CATO
AGENCY:
CATO DESIGN
■ 121, 122

■ 121, 122 For a poster issued for the occasion of the World Expo 88 in Brisbane, Australia. (AUS)

■ 121, 122 Für ein Plakat, das anlässlich der World Expo 88 in Brisbane, Australien, herausgegeben wurde. (AUS)

■ 121, 122 Pour une affiche publiée à l'occasion de la Foire universelle 88 de Brisbane, en Australie. (AUS)

PEOPLE

PERSONNES

MENSCHEN

PHOTOGRAPHER:
Marsha Burns
PUBLISHER:
Henry Art Gallery/
University of Washington
ART DIRECTOR:
Douglas Wadden
DESIGNER:
Douglas Wadden
AGENCY:
Design Collaborative
■ 123, 124

PHOTOGRAPHER:
Bruce Peterson
STUDIO:
Morse Peterson
Photography
►■ 125

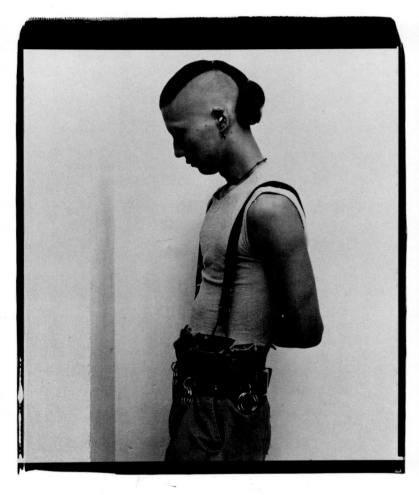

■ 123, 124 "Yaz, New York 1986" and "Kassa, New York 1986", black-and-white shots (both 61.0 x 50.8 cm) taken from the catalog for an exhibition on the subject "Cities" held at the Henry Art Gallery. (USA)

■ 125 Personal study by photographer Bruce Peterson, Boston. (USA)

■ 123, 124 Aufnahmen (beide 61,0 x 50,8 cm) mit dem Titel «Yaz, New York 1986» und «Kassa, New York 1986», aus dem Katalog für eine Ausstellung zum Thema «Städte» in der Henry Art Gallery, University of Washington. (USA)

■ 125 Persönliche Studie des Photographen Bruce Peterson, Boston. (USA)

■ 123, 124 Photos noir et blanc (61,0 x 50,8 cm). intitulées «Yaz, New York 1986» et «Kassa, New York 1986», tirées du catalogue de l'exposition des «Villes» organisée à la Henry Art Gallery de l'Université de Washington. (USA)

■ 125 Etude personnelle du photographe Bruce Peterson, Boston. (USA)

PHOTOGRAPHER:
MATTHEW ROLSTON
PUBLISHER:
ROLLING STONE
ART DIRECTOR:
FRED WOODWARD
DESIGNER:
FRED WOODWARD
■ 126

PHOTOGRAPHER:
RICHARD CROFT
PUBLISHER:
ROLLING STONE
ART DIRECTOR:
FRED WOODWARD
DESIGNER:
JOEL CUYLER
■ 127

■ 126, 127, 129 Portraits from *Rolling Stone* magazine: dancer Mikhail Baryshnikov *(126)*, science-fiction author J. G. Ballard *(127)* and former Beatle George Harrison *(129)*. (USA)

■ 128 Portrait of landscape architect Dan Kilen to accompany an article in *Peninsula Magazine.* (USA)

■ 126, 127, 129 Porträtaufnahmen aus der Zeitschrift *Rolling Stone:* der Tänzer Michail Barischnikow *(126)*, der Science-Fiction-Autor J. G. Ballard *(127)* und Ex-Beatle George Harrison *(129)*. (USA)

■ 128 Porträt des Landschaftsarchitekten Dan Kilen für einen Artikel im *Peninsula Magazine.* (USA)

■ 126, 127, 129 Portraits tirés du magazine *Rolling Stone:* le danseur Mikhaïl Barychnikov *(126)*, l'auteur de science-fiction J. G. Ballard *(127)* et l'ancien Beatle George Harrison *(129)*. (USA)

■ 128 Portrait de l'architecte-paysagiste Dan Kilen pour un article paru dans le *Peninsula Magazine.* (USA)

PHOTOGRAPHER:
RICK ENGLISH
PUBLISHER:
PENINSULA MAGAZINE
ART DIRECTOR:
DAVID GORN
■ 128

PHOTOGRAPHER:
WILLIAM COUPON
PUBLISHER:
ROLLING STONE
ART DIRECTOR:
FRED WOODWARD
DESIGNER:
FRED WOODWARD
■ 129

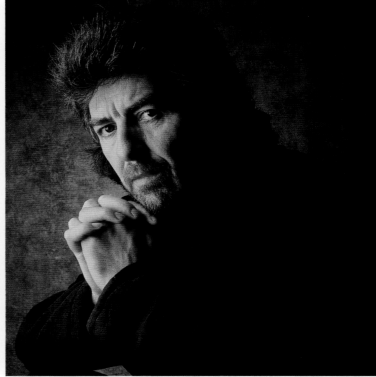

PHOTOGRAPHER:
Martin Parr
PUBLISHER:
De Geillustreerde
Pers b.v.
ART DIRECTOR:
Hans Van Blommestein
■ 130, 131

■130, 131 Photographs from the "New Brighton" series by photographer Martin Parr, to which the Dutch magazine *Avenue* devoted an article. (NLD)

■130, 131 Aufnahmen aus der «New-Brighton»-Serie des Photographen Martin Parr, dem das holländische Magazin *Avenue* einen Artikel widmete. (NLD)

■130, 131 Exemples des photos de la série «New Brighton» de Martin Parr; le magazine hollandais *Avenue* en illustre un article consacré à ce photographe. (NLD)

PHOTOGRAPHER:
JOHN CLARIDGE
PUBLISHER:
GLIMPSELAND LIMITED
ART DIRECTOR:
CHRIS LOWER
DESIGNER:
*DESIGN HOUSE
CONSULTANTS*
■ 132-134

■ 132–134 Black-and-white portraits from the book *One Hundred Photographs* by John Claridge. Shown are George Coleman, jazz musician, 1986; banjo player, Tennessee, 1986; Chet Baker, jazz musician, 1986. (GBR)

■ 132–134 Schwarzweiss-Porträts aus dem Photoband *One Hundred Photographs* des Photographen John Claridge. Hier George Coleman, Jazz-Musiker, 1986; Banjo-Spieler, Tennessee, 1986, und Chet Baker, Jazz-Musiker, 1986. (GBR)

■ 132–134 Portraits noir et blanc illustrant l'album photo *One Hundred Photographs* de John Claridge. On voit ici George Coleman, musicien de jazz, 1986; un banjoïste du Tennessee, 1986; Chet Baker, musicien de jazz, 1986. (GBR)

PHOTOGRAPHER:
Alex Chatelain
PUBLISHER:
Marie Claire
ART DIRECTOR:
Walter Rospert
■ 135-137

■135-137 "In Praise of Curves", photographs for a beauty article in the women's magazine *Marie Claire*, which deals with the new tendency towards softer lines and gives advice on how to keep them attractive. (FRA)

■135-137 «Ein Lob auf die Rundungen», Aufnahmen für einen Schönheits-Beitrag in der Frauenzeitschrift *Marie Claire*, in dem es um die neue Tendenz zu weicheren Formen und deren Pflege geht. (FRA)

■135-137 Cet «Eloge des rondeurs» dans le magazine féminin *Marie Claire* discute au chapitre de la beauté la nouvelle tendance à des formes plus épanouies et la meilleure manière de les entretenir. (FRA)

Photographer:
David Hiscock
Publisher:
Zoom
Art Director:
Joël Laroche
■ 138

■ 138 Example of the photographs by the young English photographer David Hiscock, presented in the photography magazine *Zoom.* His photographs are not only exhibited in large fashion stores but also at Madame Tussaud's. (GBR)

■ 139 Example from a series of 30 photographs entitled "Bellies", taken for an exhibition. (NLD)

■ 138 Beispiel der Aufnahmen des englischen Photographen David Hiscock, der im Photomagazin *Zoom* vorgestellt wurde. Seine Bilder sind nicht nur in grossen Modehäusern ausgestellt, sondern auch bei Madame Tussaud. (GBR)

■ 139 Aus einer Serie von 30 Aufnahmen mit dem Titel «Bäuche», die der Photograph für eine Ausstellung machte. (NLD)

■ 138 L'un des clichés du jeune photographe anglais David Hiscock présentés dans le magazine photo *Zoom.* Ses photos ne sont pas seulement exposées dans de grands magasins de modes, mais aussi chez Madame Tussaud. (GBR)

■ 139 Exemple des photos de «Ventres» réalisées par le photographe pour une exposition. (NLD)

PHOTOGRAPHER:
TAEKE HENSTRA
PUBLISHER:
ART UNLIMITED
DESIGNER:
TAEKE HENSTRA
■ 139

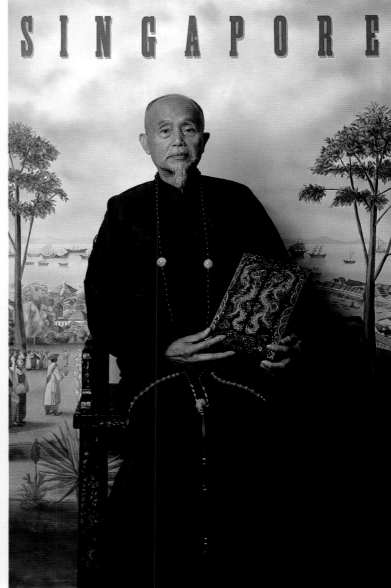

PHOTOGRAPHER:
TERRY HEFFERNAN
CLIENT:
AMERICAN PRESIDENT LINES
DESIGNER:
KIT HINRICHS
AGENCY:
PENTAGRAM
■ 140, 141

PHOTOGRAPHER:
TOM ZIMBEROFF
CLIENT:
GEORGE RICE & SONS
ART DIRECTOR:
LISA LEVIN
DESIGNER:
CROSS & ASSOCIATES
► ■ 142

■ 140, 141 Photographs used for the diary of the shipping company American President Lines. (USA)

■ 142 Portrait of a young man from the Mexican-American district of Los Angeles. He wears whatever the barrio gang dictates – whether it be a black hairnet or a pink tutu. "Be cool or be through" is the motto. (USA)

■ 140, 141 Aufnahmen für die Agenda der Reederei American President Lines. (USA)

■ 142 Porträt eines jungen Mannes aus dem mexikanischen Quartier in Los Angeles. Er ist ganz dem Modediktat seiner Quartier-Gang unterworfen: Schwarzes Haarnetz oder was immer «in» ist. (USA)

■ 140, 141 Photos illustrant l'agenda de l'armateur American President Lines. (USA)

■ 142 Portrait d'un jeune homme du quartier mexicain de Los Angeles coiffé d'un filet à cheveux noir et habillé à la mode dictée par les mouvements de jeunes de son quartier. (USA)

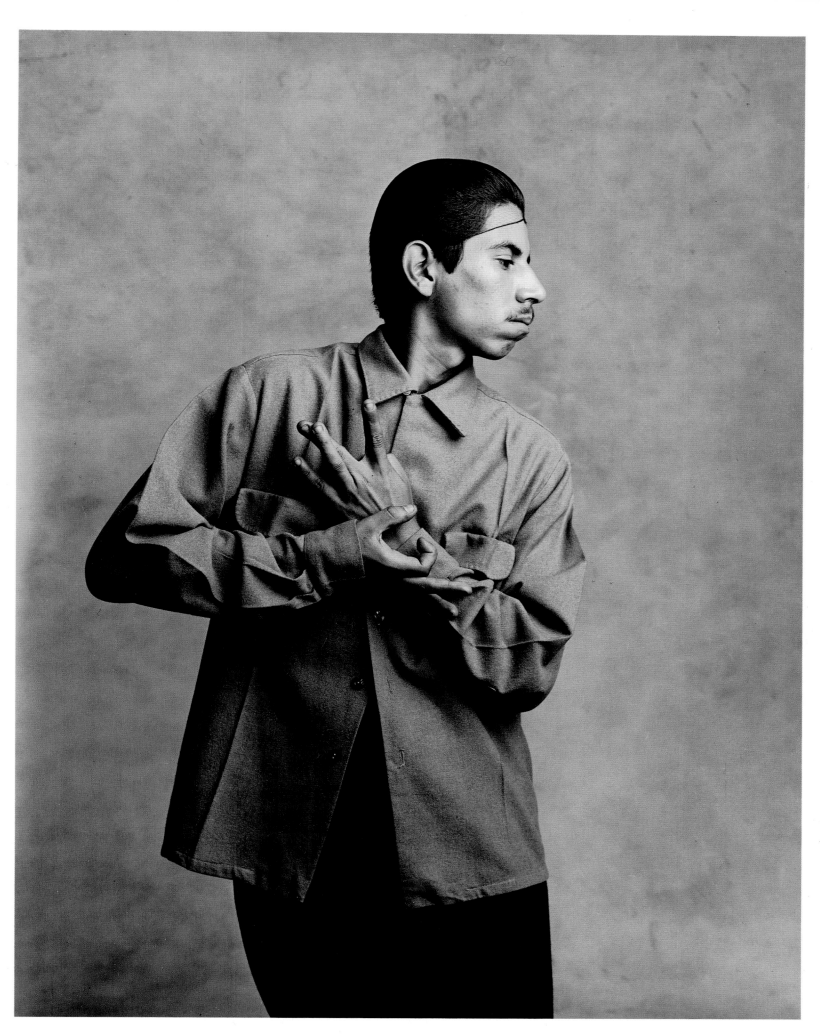

PHOTOGRAPHER:
ABE FRAJNDLICH
PUBLISHER:
FRANKFURTER ALLGEMEINE
ZEITUNG GMBH
ART DIRECTOR:
HANS-GEORG POSPISCHIL
■ 143

PHOTOGRAPHER:
CHRIS CALLIS
PUBLISHER:
ESQUIRE MAGAZINE
■ 144

PHOTOGRAPHER:
ALBERT WATSON
PUBLISHER:
ROLLING STONE
ART DIRECTOR:
FRED WOODWARD
►■ 145

■ 143 From an article in the *Frankfurter Allgemeine Magazin* on the famous French film director Louis Malle. (USA)

■ 144 Ray Charles and Peter Martins, photograph published in the magazine *Esquire*. (USA)

■ 145 Portrait of Keith Richards for an article in *Rolling Stone* magazine. (USA)

■ 143 Aus einem Artikel über den französischen Filmregisseur Louis Malle im *Frankfurter Allgemeine Magazin*. (GER)

■ 144 Ray Charles und Peter Martins, Aufnahme für die Zeitschrift *Esquire*. (USA)

■ 145 Porträtaufnahme von Keith Richards aus der Zeitschrift *Rolling Stone*. (USA)

■ 143 D'un article du *Frankfurter Allgemeine Magazin* sur le grand régisseur de films français Louis Malle. (GER)

■ 144 Ray Charles et Peter Martins, photo publiée dans le magazine *Esquire*. (USA)

■ 145 Portrait de Keith Richards pour un article paru dans le magazine *Rolling Stone*. (USA)

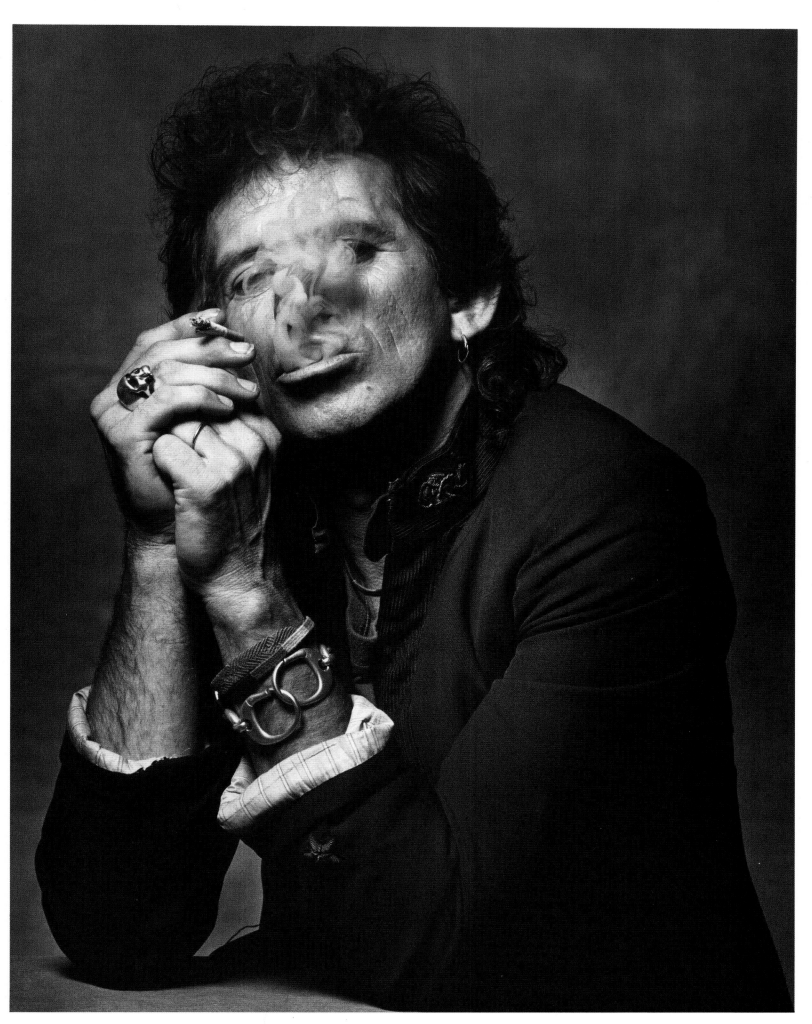

PHOTOGRAPHER:
J. K. Lee
PUBLISHER:
Minolta Camera Co. Ltd.
ART DIRECTOR:
Fred O. Bechlen
■ 146

PHOTOGRAPHER:
BARBARA BORDNICK
PUBLISHER:
SELECT MAGAZINE
ART DIRECTOR:
BARBARA BORDNICK
DESIGNER:
BARBARA BORDNICK
STUDIO:
BARBARA BORDNICK
■ 147

PHOTOGRAPHER:
HERMANN FÖRSTERLING
PUBLISHER:
PHOTOGRAPHIE
ART DIRECTOR:
PETER WASSERMANN
■ 148

■ 146 A 23-year-old Korean girl with dried flowers – nude portrait taken by J. K. Lee, with amber diffusing filter, *Kodacolor VR 1000* film, and natural lighting. From the magazine *Minolta Mirror.* (JPN)

■ 147 New York photographer Barbara Bordnick uses this shot as self-promotion. (USA)

■ 148 Basic material for this unique photograph is a black-and-white nude shot enlarged on 50 x 60 cm baryta paper. A selenium toning gives the skin its silver effect. The colors are applied by brush, palette knife, and airbrush. From *Portfolio Photographie.* (SWI)

■ 146 Akt eines 23jährigen koreanischen Mädchens mit Trockenblumen, aufgenommen von J. K. Lee mit Bernsteinfilter, *Kodacolor-VR-1000*-Film, bei natürlichem Licht. Aus der Zeitschrift *Minolta Mirror.* (JPN)

■ 147 Als Eigenwerbung verwendete Aufnahme der New Yorker Photographin Barbara Bordnick. (USA)

■ 148 Ausgangsmaterial für dieses Unikatbild ist eine schwarzweisse Aktaufnahme, auf 50 x 60 cm Barytpapier vergrössert. Eine Selentonung verleiht der Haut den Silbereffekt. Die Farben werden mit Pinsel, Spachtel und Airbrush aufgetragen. Aus *Portfolio Photographie.* (SWI)

■ 146 Nu (Coréenne de 23 ans) avec des fleurs séchées. Photo de J. K. Lee utilisant un filtre ambré, un film *Kodacolor VR 1000* et l'éclairage naturel. Cette photo a paru dans le magazine *Minolta Mirror.* (JPN)

■ 147 Photo que la photographe new-yorkaise Barbara Bordnick utilise pour sa promotion personnelle. (USA)

■ 148 Le point départ de ce tirage unique est un nu noir et blanc agrandi sur papier de baryte de 50 x 60 cm. Un virage au sélénium confère à la peau un éclat argenté. Les couleurs sont appliquées au pinceau, au couteau et à l'aérographe. Paru dans *Portfolio Photographie.* (SWI)

PHOTOGRAPHER:
LEE CRUM
ART DIRECTOR:
LEE CRUM
■ 149

■149 Self-promotion by photographer Lee Crum. (USA)

■150 "Odalisque" is the title of this personal study by photographer Jody Dole. (USA)

■149 Eigenwerbung des Photographen Lee Crum. (USA)

■150 «Odaliske» ist der Titel dieser persönlichen Studie des Photographen Jody Dole. (USA)

■149 Autopromotion du photographe Lee Crum. (USA)

■150 Cette «Odalisque» est une étude personnelle du photographe Jody Dole. (USA)

PHOTOGRAPHER:
JODY DOLE
ART DIRECTOR:
JODY DOLE
■150

PHOTOGRAPHER:
TOM LEVY
PUBLISHER:
SAN FRANCISCO CHRONICLE
■ 151

PHOTOGRAPHER:
WILL VAN OVERBEEK
PUBLISHER:
TEXAS MONTHLY
ART DIRECTOR:
NANCY E. McMILLEN
DESIGNER:
NANCY E. McMILLEN
■ 152

■ 151 Portrait of photographer and film maker Robert Frank, taken in a Greyhound Bus Station, for an article in the *San Francisco Chronicle*. (USA)

■ 152 Portrait shot to accompany an article in the *Texas Monthly:* Bert Turner, funeral home greeter. (USA)

■ 151 Porträt des Photographen und Filmemachers Robert Frank, aufgenommen in einer Greyhound-Busstation, für einen Beitrag im *San Francisco Chronicle*. (USA)

■ 152 Porträtaufnahme für einen Beitrag in *Texas Monthly:* Bert Turner, Angestellter eines Beerdigungsinstituts. (USA)

■ 151 Portrait du photographe et cinéaste Robert Frank, capté dans une gare des autobus Greyhound pour un article du *San Francisco Chronicle*. (USA)

■ 152 Portrait pour un article du *Texas Monthly:* Bert Turner, un employé des pompes funèbres. (USA)

PHOTOGRAPHER:
Annie Leibovitz
CLIENT:
American Express Co.
ART DIRECTOR:
Parry Merkley
AGENCY:
Ogilvy and Mather
■ 153–159

■ 153–159 Examples of some of the unusual portraits of people (all famous in the USA) used for an advertising campaign by American Express. Shown are: actress Candice Bergen, skier Billy Kidd, Ella Fitzgerald, James Earl Jones, actor, speed-skater Eric Heiden, Willie Shoemaker, jockey, and Wilt Chamberlain, former baseball player, as well as Beth Henley, playwright. (USA)

■ 153–159 Porträts von in den USA berühmten Leuten, die für eine Inseratenkampagne von American Express verwendet wurden. Hier die Schauspielerin Candice Bergen, Skiläufer Billy Kidd, Ella Fitzgerald, James Earl Jones, Schauspieler, Eisschnelläufer Eric Heiden, Willie Shoemaker, Jockey, und Wilt Chamberlain, ehemaliger Baseball-Spieler, sowie Beth Henley, Dramatikerin. (USA)

■ 153–159 Exemples des portraits extraordinaires de personnalités de tout premier plan utilisés pour une campagne d'annonces de l'American Express. On voit ici l'actrice Candice Bergen, le skieur Billy Kidd, Ella Fitzgerald, le comédien James Earl Jones, le patineur de vitesse Eric Heiden, le jockey Willie Shoemaker avec l'ancien joueur de base-ball Wilt Chamberlain et la dramaturge Beth Henley. (USA)

PHOTOGRAPHER:
ANNIE LEIBOVITZ
CLIENT:
AMERICAN EXPRESS CO.
ART DIRECTOR:
PARRY MERKLEY
AGENCY:
OGILVY AND MATHER
■ 160–163

■ 160–163 From a series of unusual portraits of personalities famous in the USA, taken by Annie Leibovitz for an advertising campaign for American Express. Shown are the sprinter Evelyn Ashford, football star John Elway, the comedian Alan King, and Helen Hayes, actress. (USA)

■ 160–163 Aus einer Reihe von aussergewöhnlichen Porträts, die Annie Leibovitz für eine Werbekampagne von American Express machte. Hier die Sprinterin Evelyn Ashford, der Football-Spieler John Elway, der Komiker Alan King und Helen Hayes, Schauspielerin. (USA)

■ 160–163 Exemples des portraits exceptionnels réalisés par Annie Leibovitz pour une campagne publicitaire de l'American Express: la sprinter Evelyn Ashford, le joueur de football John Elway, le comique Alan King et la comédienne Helen Hayes. (USA)

■ 164 Portrait of rock/pop singer Paul Simon (formerly of Simon & Garfunkel) for an article in *Vogue Italia*. (ITA)

■ 165 Grace Jones on the sleeve of her album "Slave to the Rhythm", taken by Jean-Paul Goude. (FRA)

■ 164 Porträt des Rock-Sängers Paul Simon (früher «Simon & Garfunkel») für einen Beitrag in *Vogue Italia*. (ITA)

■ 165 Grace Jones für die Hülle ihrer Schallplatte «Slave to the Rhythm», aufgenommen von Jean-Paul Goude. (FRA)

■ 164 Portrait du chanteur rock et pop Paul Simon autrefois associé à Garfunkel, pour un article de *Vogue Italia*. (ITA)

■ 165 Grace Jones sur la pochette de son disque «Slave to the Rhythm», photographiée par Jean-Paul Goude. (FRA)

PHOTOGRAPHER:
WILLIAM COUPON
CLIENT:
VOGUE ITALIA
PUBLISHER:
CONDÉ NAST S.P.A.
ART DIRECTOR:
ALBERTO NODOLINI
◄ ■ 164

PHOTOGRAPHER:
JEAN-PAUL GOUDE
PUBLISHER:
ISLAND INTERNATIONAL
DESIGNER:
JEAN-PAUL GOUDE
STUDIO:
ISLAND RECORDS
■ 165

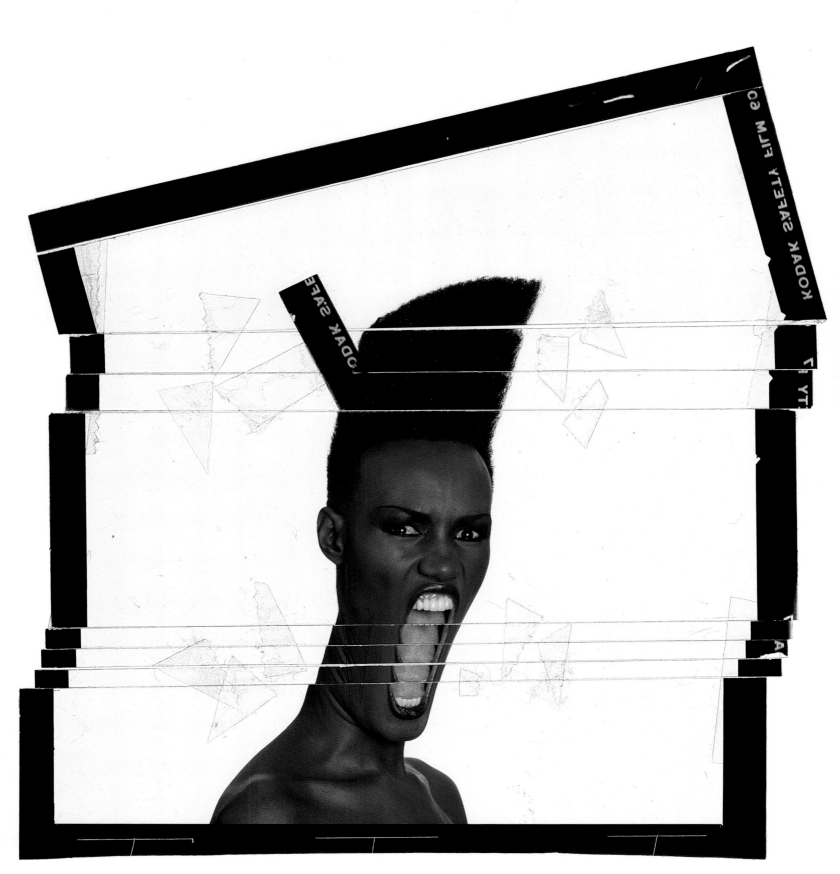

PHOTOGRAPHER:
DEBORAH ROUNDTREE
PUBLISHER:
LA BONNE IDÉE
ART DIRECTOR:
DEBORAH ROUNDTREE
DESIGNER:
RENÉE WARD
■ 166, 167

■ 166, 167 Shots taken for fashion accessories. (FRA)

■ 168 Nude shot for an article on Czech photographer Jan Saudek in *Minolta Mirror*. For all his esthetics, this photographer does not shy at a bit of fun. (JPN)

■ 166, 167 Aufnahmen für Mode-Accessoires. (FRA)

■ 168 Aktaufnahme aus einem Artikel über den tschechischen Photographen Jan Saudek in *Minolta Mirror*. Bei aller Ästhetik verzichtet er nicht auf ein bisschen Humor. (JPN)

■ 166, 167 Photos pour des accessoires de mode. (FRA)

■ 168 Nu illustrant un article du magazine *Minolta Mirror* sur le photographe tchèque Jan Saudek. La recherche de l'esthétique ne nuit pas à la qualité de l'humour. (JPN)

PHOTOGRAPHER:
Jan Saudek
PUBLISHER:
Minolta Camera Co. Ltd.
ART DIRECTOR:
Fred O. Bechlen
■ 168

■169, 170 Photographs from an article appearing in Audi of America's house magazine *Spirit of Audi*, featuring a driving tour of Albuquerque, Santa Fe and Taos, New Mexico. Shown is a shy three-year-old eagle dancer, and a fellow dancer in traditional buffalo regalia. (USA)

■171 A photograph used for the announcement of a lecture by photographer Jay Maisel. (USA)

■169, 170 Albuquerque, Santa Fe und Taos in Neumexiko sind die Stationen einer Fahrt, die in der Hauszeitschrift von Audi of America beschrieben wird. Hier ein etwas schüchterner, dreijähriger Adler-Tänzer und ein weiterer Tänzer mit den traditionellen Buffalo-Insignien. (USA)

■171 Für die Ankündigung eines Vortrages des Photographen Jay Maisel verwendete Aufnahme. (USA)

■169, 170 Albuquerque, Santa Fe et Taos au Nouveau-Mexique, étapes d'un voyage décrit dans la revue d'entreprise d'Audi of America. Les photos montrent un danseur à l'aigle un peu timide, âgé de 3 ans, ainsi qu'un autre danseur arborant les traditionnels insignes de buffles. (USA)

■171 Photo utilisée pour l'annonce d'une conférence par le photographe Jay Maisel. (USA)

PHOTOGRAPHER:
RODNEY RASCONA
CLIENT:
AUDI OF AMERICA, INC.
ART DIRECTOR:
MILES ABERNETHY
DESIGNER:
MILES ABERNETHY
STUDIO:
*SHR COMMUNICATIONS
PLANNING & DESIGN*
◄■ 169, 170

PHOTOGRAPHER:
JAY MAISEL
PUBLISHER:
ASMP
ART DIRECTOR:
JANE LANGA
AGENCY:
*NOT JUST AN
ART DIRECTOR'S CLUB*
■ 171

■ 172 Experimental work belonging to a series by photographer William G.Wagner. (USA)

■ 173 Photograph by New York photographer Hans Neleman for Kodak U.K. (GBR)

■ 172 Experimentelle Arbeit des Photographen William G.Wagner, die zu einer Serie gehört. (USA)

■ 173 Aufnahme des New Yorker Photographen Hans Neleman für Kodak U.K. (GBR)

■ 172 Réalisation expérimentale du photographe William G.Wagner faisant partie de toute une série. (USA)

■ 173 Photo du photographe new-yorkais Hans Neleman pour une promotion de Kodak U.K. (GBR)

PHOTOGRAPHER:
WILLIAM G. WAGNER
◄ ■ 172

PHOTOGRAPHER:
HANS NELEMAN
CLIENT:
KODAK U.K.
ART DIRECTOR:
PAUL WIGMORE
■ 173

PHOTOGRAPHER:
JOE BARABAN
CLIENT:
MAINE PHOTOGRAPHIC
WORKSHOP
ART DIRECTOR:
JOE BARABAN
DESIGNER:
JOE BARABAN
■ 174

PHOTOGRAPHER:
JIM KRANTZ
CLIENT:
REGAL PRINTING CO.
DESIGNER:
DAN HATFIELD
AGENCY:
GALEN & NELLIE INC.
■ 175

PHOTOGRAPHER:
HERB RITTS
PUBLISHER:
ROLLING STONE
ART DIRECTOR:
FRED WOODWARD
DESIGNER:
FRED WOODWARD
► ■ 176

■ 174 By this photo of a man in "Popeye" costume the photographer wants to demonstrate the influence of light. It is used by him for teaching purposes. (USA)

■ 175 Photograph used as advertising for a printers. (USA)

■ 176 Portrait to accompany an article on Madonna in *Rolling Stone* magazine. (USA)

■ 174 Mit dieser Aufnahme eines Mannes im «Popeye»-Kostüm will der Photograph den Einfluss des Lichtes demonstrieren. Er verwendet sie für Unterrichtszwecke. (USA)

■ 175 Aufnahme als Werbung für eine Druckerei. (USA)

■ 176 Porträt für einen Beitrag über Madonna in der Zeitschrift *Rolling Stone*. (USA)

■ 174 Par le biais de cette photo d'un homme en costume de «Popeye», le photographe veut démontrer l'influence de la lumière. Cette photo lui sert pour son enseignement. (USA)

■ 175 Photo utilisée pour la publicité d'un imprimeur. (USA)

■ 176 Portrait pour un article du magazine *Rolling Stone* consacré à Madonna. (USA)

PHOTOGRAPHER:
ABE FRAJNDLICH
PUBLISHER:
*FRANKFURTER ALLGEMEINE
ZEITUNG GMBH*
ART DIRECTOR:
HANS-GEORG POSPISCHIL
■ 177

PHOTOGRAPHER:
KENT BARKER
PUBLISHER:
REGARDIE'S
ART DIRECTOR:
FRED WOODWARD
DESIGNER:
JOEL CUYLER
► ■ 178

■ 177 Portrait of interior architect Andrée Putman, shown here with a lamp created by the Italian Mariano Fortuny, that she rediscovered and reproduced. From an article in the *Frankfurter Allgemeine Magazin.* (GER)

■ 178 "Dan and Pat Moore, 18". Shot from a series devoted to cyclists, taken by photographer Kent Barker and published in *Regardie's* magazine. (USA)

■ 177 Porträt der Innenarchitektin Andrée Putman, hier mit einer Lampe des Italieners Mariano Fortuny, die sie wiederentdeckt und nachgebaut hat. Aus einem Artikel im *Frankfurter Allgemeine Magazin.* (GER)

■ 178 «Dan und Pat Moore, 18», Aufnahme aus einer Serie des Photographen Kent Barker, die Radfahrern gewidmet ist und in der Zeitschrift *Regardie's* veröffentlicht wurde. (USA)

■ 177 Portrait de l'ensemblière-décoratrice Andrée Putman avec une lampe de l'Italien Mariano Fortuny qu'elle a redécouverte et copiée. Photo illustrant un article publié dans le *Frankfurter Allgemeine Magazin.* (GER)

■ 178 «Dan et Pat Moore, 18» – photo réalisée par Kent Barker pour une série vouée au cyclisme et publiée dans le magazine *Regardie's.* (USA)

PHOTOGRAPHER:
FRANCIS GIACOBETTI
PUBLISHER:
CAMERA INTERNATIONAL
ART DIRECTOR:
GABRIEL BAURET
■ 179

PHOTOGRAPHER:
John Chan
PUBLISHER:
Taxi Magazine
DESIGNER:
John Chan
■ 180

■ 179 Photograph by Francis Giacobetti, from an article about this photographer in *Camera* magazine. (FRA)

■ 180 Photograph to be included in the "Beauty" column of *Taxi* magazine. (USA)

■ 179 Aufnahme von Francis Giacobetti, aus einem Beitrag über diesen Photographen in der Zeitschrift *Camera*. (FRA)

■ 180 Für die Rubrik «Schönheit» des *Taxi*-Magazins verwendete Aufnahme. (USA)

■ 179 Photo de Francis Giacobetti reprise dans un article du magazine *Camera* pour ce photographe. (FRA)

■ 180 Photo utilisée pour la rubrique Beauté du magazine *Taxi*. (USA)

PHOTOGRAPHER:
Robert van der Hilst
PUBLISHER:
Zoom
ART DIRECTOR:
Joël Laroche
■181

PHOTOGRAPHER:
KAM HINATSU
ART DIRECTOR:
KAM HINATSU
■ 182

■ 181 Example from a series of photographs by Robert van der Hilst, taken in Marocco and published in *Zoom* photo magazine. (FRA)

■ 182 Black-and-white photo used as self-promotion by Kam Hinatsu. (USA)

■ 181 Beispiel aus einer Serie von Aufnahmen des Photographen Robert van der Hilst, die in Marokko entstanden sind und im Photo-Magazin *Zoom* veröffentlicht wurden. (FRA)

■ 182 Als Eigenwerbung verwendete Schwarzweissaufnahme des Photographen Kam Hinatsu. (USA)

■ 181 Exemple de la série de photos réalisée au Maroc par le photographe Robert van der Hilst et publiée dans le magazine photo *Zoom*. (FRA)

■ 182 Photo noir et blanc autopromotionnelle du photographe Kam Hinatsu. (USA)

PHOTOGRAPHER:
DAVID HISCOCK
PUBLISHER:
ZOOM
ART DIRECTOR:
JOËL LAROCHE
◀ ■183

■183 From a series of shots by English photographer David Hiscock, presented in *Zoom* photo magazine. (FRA)

■183 Aus einer Reihe von Aufnahmen des englischen Photographen David Hiscock, der in *Zoom* vorgestellt wurde. (FRA)

■183 Photo figurant dans une série de prises de vues de l'Anglais David Hiscock que le magazine *Zoom* présente à ses lecteurs. (FRA)

PHOTOGRAPHER:
DENIS CHAPOULLIÉ
PUBLISHER:
CAMERA INTERNATIONAL
ART DIRECTOR:
GABRIEL BAURET
■184

■184 Portrait of a young woman by Denis Chapoullié, who showed his photographs at the "Off" presentation at the "Rencontres d'Arles" event. From *Camera* magazine. (FRA)

■184 Porträt einer jungen Frau von Denis Chapoullié, der seine Bilder bei den «Off»-Vorführungen anlässlich der «Rencontres d'Arles» zeigte. Aus der Zeitschrift *Camera*. (FRA)

■184 Portrait d'une jeune femme par Denis Chapoullié, qui a présenté ses créations en marge des Rencontres d'Arles. Extrait du magazine *Camera*. (FRA)

■ 185 Black-and-white shots as self-promotion for photographer Benjamin Franklin Smith. Model: Craig Uher. (USA)

■ 186 One of a series of outstanding pictures by photographers working with *Kodak Professional Film* and presented in *International Photography.* For this photographic reproduction of Pieter Brueghel's *The Wedding Feast* 48 000 footcandles of electronic flash, 35 models, and countless propmakers, stylists, make up artists, and set builders were required. Preparations took 4 months. Originally used to promote the Holland Cheese Exporters Agency. (USA)

■ 185 Schwarzweissaufnahmen als Eigenwerbung von Benjamin Franklin Smith. Modell: Craig Uher. (USA)

■ 186 Aus einer Reihe hervorragender Bilder von Photographen, die mit *Kodak Professional Film* arbeiten, vorgestellt in *International Photography.* Für diese photographische Reproduktion von Pieter Brueghels *Bauernhochzeit* waren elektronisches Blitzlicht in einer Stärke von ca. 500 000 Lux sowie zahlreiche Maskenbildner, Stylisten und Dekorateure notwendig. Ursprünglicher Auftraggeber war ein holländischer Käse-Exporteur. (USA)

■ 185 Photos noir et blanc autopromotionnelles de Benjamin Franklin Smith. Son modèle s'appelle Craig Uher. (USA)

■ 186 Photo présentée dans *International Photography* dans le cadre d'une collection de photos exceptionnelles par des artistes utilisant le film *Kodak Professional.* Pour cette photoreproduction de *La Noce* de Pieter Bruegel l'Ancien, on a utilisé un flash électronique de quelque 500 000 lx, ainsi qu'une armée de maquilleurs, de stylistes et de décorateurs. Cette photo a servi au départ pour l'affiche d'un exportateur de fromages hollandais. (USA)

PHOTOGRAPHER:
BENJAMIN FRANKLIN SMITH
PUBLISHER:
SELECT MAGAZINE
ART DIRECTOR:
BENJAMIN FRANKLIN SMITH
DESIGNER:
BENJAMIN FRANKLIN SMITH
AGENCY:
BENJAMIN FRANKLIN SMITH
PHOTOGRAPHY
◄ ■ 185

PHOTOGRAPHER:
BERT BELL
PUBLISHER:
EASTMAN KODAK COMPANY
ART DIRECTOR:
STEPHEN HALL
AGENCY:
RUMRILL-HOYT, INC.
■ 186

PHOTOGRAPHER:
ALBERT WATSON
PUBLISHER:
ROLLING STONE
ART DIRECTOR:
FRED WOODWARD
DESIGNER:
FRED WOODWARD
◄ ■ 187

■ 187 Portrait of actress Ellen Barkin, that appeared in *Rolling Stone* magazine under the column "New Faces". (USA)

■ 187 Porträt der Schauspielerin Ellen Barkin, die unter der Rubrik «Neue Gesichter» in *Rolling Stone* vorgestellt wurde. (USA)

■ 187 Portrait de la comédienne Ellen Barkin, présenté dans la rubrique «Nouveaux Visages» du magazine *Rolling Stone.* (USA)

PHOTOGRAPHER:
STAN KEARL
■ 188–190

■ 188–190 "Vibrance of Stilled Motion", photographs from a series of personal studies by photographer Stan Kearl. (USA)

■ 188–190 Beispiele aus einer Reihe persönlicher Studien des Photographen Stan Kearl mit einer Tänzerin. (USA)

■ 188–190 Exemples d'études personnelles dans une série du photographe Stan Kearl avec une danseuse pour modèle. (USA)

PHOTOGRAPHER:
RICK ENGLISH
■ 191

PHOTOGRAPHER:
JEAN-PAUL GOUDE
STYLIST:
*PATRICK FÜR JACQUES MOISANT
(HAIR)/YASEMINE (MAKE-UP)*
CLIENT:
MÄNNER VOGUE
PUBLISHER:
CONDÉ NAST VERLAG GMBH
ART DIRECTOR:
BEDA ACHERMANN
■ 192

PHOTOGRAPHER:
François Gillet
CLIENT:
Nakatsuka Daisuke Inc.
ART DIRECTOR:
Daisuke Nakatsuka
DESIGNER:
Masato Isobe
AGENCY:
Nakatsuka Daisuke Inc.
■ 193

PHOTOGRAPHER:
Darrell Peterson
PUBLISHER:
Oceanic Poster Company
ART DIRECTOR:
Darrell Peterson
DESIGNER:
William Allen
AGENCY:
William Allen and Assoc.
► ■ 194

■193 The Japanese ad agency Nakatsuka Daisuke Inc. uses this photograph as a self-promotional poster with the slogan: "We take pleasure in creating pleasure". (JPN)

■194 Poster on general sale, showing Cory Everson, bodybuilder: "Miss Olympia". (USA)

■193 Die japanische Werbeagentur Nakatsuka Daisuke Inc. verwendete diese Aufnahme für ein Eigenwerbungsplakat: «Es macht uns Vergnügen, Vergnügen zu bereiten». (JPN)

■194 Im Handel erhältliches Plakat mit Bodybuilderin Cory Everson: «Miss Olympia». (USA)

■193 L'agence de publicité japonaise, Nakatsuka Daisuke Inc. a utilisé cette photo pour une affiche autopromotionnelle: «Nous avons du plaisir à faire plaisir». (JPN)

■194 Affiche «Miss Olympia» de la culturiste Cory Everson, libérée pour la vente. (USA)

PHOTOGRAPHER:
HERB RITTS
PUBLISHER:
ROLLING STONE
ART DIRECTOR:
FRED WOODWARD
DESIGNER:
JOEL CUYLER
■ 195

■ 195 Portrait of film director John Huston who died in 1987, published in *Rolling Stone* magazine. (USA)

■ 195 Im Gedenken an den 1987 verstorbenen Filmregisseur John Huston veröffentlichtes Porträt in *Rolling Stone*. (USA)

■ 195 Portrait du cinéaste John Huston décédé en 1987 publié dans *Rolling Stone*. (USA)

ANIMAUX

TIERE

PHOTOGRAPHER:
ANSELM SPRING
PUBLISHER:
FRANKFURTER ALLGEMEINE
ZEITUNG GMBH
ART DIRECTOR:
HANS-GEORG POSPISCHIL
■ 196

■ 196 From an article on Ireland in the *Frankfurter Allgemeine Magazin.* Irish ballads recount the tales of people magically transfigured into the forms of animals. (GER)

■ 197 Adélie penguins on the Antarctic's eternal ice. Despite their seeming awkwardness in running, a human being can barely catch up with them. Photo published in the *Stern* magazine. (GER)

■ 196 Aufnahme aus einem Artikel über Irland im *Frankfurter Allgemeine Magazin:* Die irischen Lieder erzählen von verzauberten Menschen in Tiergestalt. (GER)

■ 197 Zwei Adéliepinguine im ewigen Eis der Antarktis. Trotz der scheinbaren Tolpatschigkeit laufen sie so schnell, dass ein Mensch kaum folgen könnte. Aus dem Magazin *Stern.* (GER)

■ 196 D'un article que le *Frankfurter Allgemeine Magazin* consacre à l'Irlande. Référence aux êtres humains errant dans un corps d'animal, dans les chansons du folklore. (GER)

■ 197 Deux pingouins de la terre Adélie dans les glaces éternelles de l'Antarctique. Ces palmipèdes maladroits en apparence courent plus vite que l'homme. Extrait du magazine *Stern.* (GER)

PHOTOGRAPHER:
Bruno J. Zehnder
PUBLISHER:
Gruner + Jahr AG & Co.
ART DIRECTOR:
Manfred Roser
DESIGNER:
Reinald Blanck
■ 197

PHOTOGRAPHER:
JOHN CLARIDGE
PUBLISHER:
GLIMPSELAND LIMITED
ART DIRECTOR:
CHRIS LOWER
DESIGNER:
DESIGN HOUSE CONSULTANTS
■ 198

■ 198 "Dead Gannet, 1984". Black-and-white photograph from the book *One Hundred Photographs* by John Claridge, published by Glimpseland Ltd. (GBR)

■ 198 Ein toter Tölpel, Schwarzweiss-Aufnahme aus dem Buch *One Hundred Photographs* von John Claridge, erschienen bei Glimpseland Ltd. (GBR)

■ 198 Cadavre d'un fou de Bassan. Photo noir et blanc tirée de l'album *One Hundred Photographs* de John Claridge, publié par Glimpseland Ltd. (GBR)

INDUSTRIE / PRODUKTE

■ 199 Photograph for the cover of a special issue of *Bicycle Magazine*. (USA)

■ 200 Photograph of a *Honda* for an agenda. (USA)

■ 201 The *Paso 750* as used by the photographer R. J. Muna for his own promotion. (USA)

■ 199 Aufnahme für den Umschlag einer Sonderausgabe des Sportmagazins *Bicycle*. (USA)

■ 200 Aufnahme einer *Honda* für eine Agenda. (USA)

■ 201 Als Eigenwerbung des Photographen R. J. Muna verwendete Aufnahme einer *Paso 750*. (USA)

■ 199 Photo pour la couverture d'un numéro spécial du magazine sportif *Bicycle*. (USA)

■ 200 Photo d'une moto *Honda* pour un agenda. (USA)

■ 201 Photo d'une moto *Paso 750* que son auteur, R. J. Muna, utilise pour sa publicité personnelle. (USA)

PHOTOGRAPHER:
David Holt
CLIENT:
Bicycle Magazine
PUBLISHER:
Rodale Press
ART DIRECTOR:
Sally Ulman/David Holt
DESIGNER:
Sally Ulman
◄■ 199

PHOTOGRAPHER:
Jon Kubly
CLIENT:
Fox & Clark
ART DIRECTOR:
Rebecca Mendez Vianu
(Calendar)
Tom Saputo (Photo)
DESIGNER:
Rebecca Mendez Vianu
AGENCY:
Vianu Design
■ 200

PHOTOGRAPHER:
RJ Muna
■ 201

PHOTOGRAPHER:
Curt Fischer
CLIENT:
Bianchi USA Inc.
ART DIRECTOR:
Gene Icardi
DESIGNER:
Gene Icardi
AGENCY:
Gene Icardi & Associates
◀■ 202

PHOTOGRAPHER:
Bruno Joachim
CLIENT:
Bruno Joachim Studio, Inc.
ART DIRECTOR:
Bruno Joachim
■ 203

■ 202 Photograph published in many cycling magazines in the USA and used by the photographer Curt Fischer, San Francisco, for his own promotion. (USA)

■ 203 "Black Car", hand-colored photograph used by the Bruno Joachim Studio for its own promotion. (USA)

■ 202 In den meisten Fahrradmagazinen der USA veröffentlichte Aufnahme, die auch als Eigenwerbung des Photographen Curt Fischer, San Francisco, verwendet wurde. (USA)

■ 203 «Schwarzes Auto», handkolorierte Aufnahme als Eigenwerbung des Bruno-Joachim-Studios. (USA)

■ 202 Photo publiée dans la plupart des magazines routiers et utilisée par le photographe Curt Fischer de San Francisco pour sa publicité personnelle. (USA)

■ 203 «Auto noire», photo coloriée main servant à l'auto-promotion du studio Bruno Joachim. (USA)

PHOTOGRAPHER:
DIETMAR HENNEKA
CLIENT:
DR. ING. H.C. F. PORSCHE AG
ART DIRECTOR:
GÜNTHER TIBI
AGENCY:
WENSAUER & PARTNER
■ 204, 205

PHOTOGRAPHER:
DIETMAR HENNEKA
CLIENT:
MERCEDES-BENZ OF
NORTH AMERICA, INC.
ART DIRECTOR:
GUNTHER MAIER
AGENCY:
McCAFFREY & McCALL
►■ 206

■ 204, 205 *"Porsche, Driving at its Most Beautiful".* From an advertising campaign for *Porsche* sports car. (GER)

■ 206 A 1936 *Mercedes 540K* as used in an advertising campaign for Mercedes-Benz of North America. (USA)

■ 204, 205 Für eine *Porsche*-Werbekampagne unter dem Motto *»Porsche, Fahren in seiner schönsten Form».* (GER)

■ 206 Ein *Mercedes 540K* von 1936, aufgenommen für eine Werbekampagne der Mercedes-Benz of North America. (USA)

■ 204, 205 Photos pour la campagne publicitaire de *Porsche* intitulée *«Porsche, la conduite sous sa forme idéale».* (GER)

■ 206 *Mercedes 540K* de 1936. Photo pour une campagne publicitaire de Mercedes-Benz of North America. (USA)

■ 207–210 "Working with the Environment". Photographs from a brochure issued by the *Audi* dealers of North America. (USA)

■ 207–210 Aufnahmen aus einer Broschüre der nordamerikanischen *Audi*-Händler mit dem Titel «Mit der Umwelt arbeiten». (USA)

■ 207–210 Pour une brochure des distributeurs *Audi* d'Amérique du Nord intitulée «Travailler avec l'environnement». (USA)

PHOTOGRAPHER:
RICK RUSING
CLIENT:
AUDI OF AMERICA
ART DIRECTOR:
BARRY SHEPARD
DESIGNER:
KARIN BURKLEIN ARNOLD
AGENCY:
SHR COMMUNICATIONS
■ 207–210

PHOTOGRAPHER:
BERNHARD LEHN
CLIENT:
*MESSERSCHMITT-BÖLKOW-
BLOHM GmbH*
ART DIRECTOR:
NORBERT HÖCHTLEN
DESIGNER:
NORBERT HÖCHTLEN
AGENCY:
WESTERMAIR & HARTWIG
■ 211–213

■ 211–213 Photographs from a calendar showing the *Tornado* and a helicopter, belonging to the manufacturing program of the MBB aircraft company. (GER)

■ 214 From a brochure published by the Loral Corporation. The photograph refers to the wheel and brake systems for the *F-4 Phantom*. (USA)

■ 211–213 Die *Tornado* und ein Hubschrauber sind Gegenstand dieser Aufnahmen aus einem Kalender für MBB-Flugzeugbau und Teil des Herstellungsprogramms. (GER)

■ 214 Aus einer Firmenbroschüre für Loral Corporation. Die Aufnahme bezieht sich auf die Reifen- und Bremssysteme der *F-4 Phantom*. (USA)

■ 211–213 Le *Tornado* et un hélicoptère sont les thèmes de ces photos tirées du calendrier mural du constructeur d'avions MBB. (GER)

■ 214 Brochure de présentation de la Loral Corporation. La photo se réfère aux systèmes d'atterrissage et de freinage du *F-4 Phantom*. (USA)

PHOTOGRAPHER:
FREDERICK SUTTER

CLIENT:
LORAL CORPORATION

ART DIRECTOR:
EDWARD BRODERICK

DESIGNER:
*EDWARD BRODERICK/
CAROLYN ECKERT/
ELIZABETH SMALL-HILDEBRANDT*

AGENCY:
PELLEGRINI AND ASSOC., INC.

▶ ■ 214

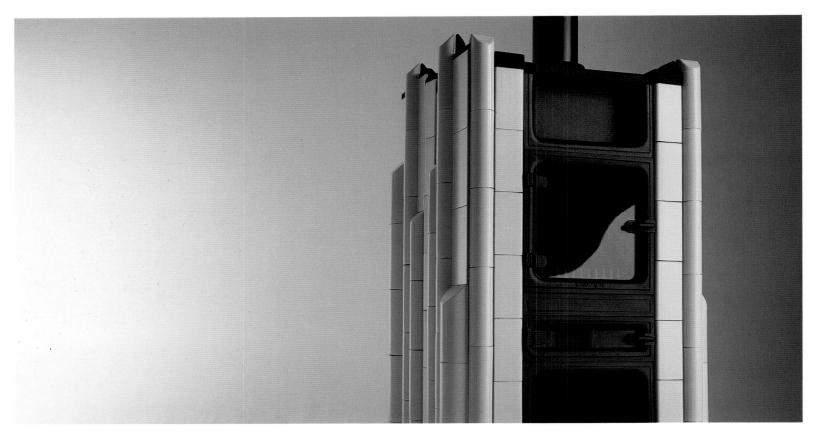

PHOTOGRAPHER:
FRANK EXNER
CLIENT:
PRO INDUSTRIA
ART DIRECTOR:
HANS GÜNTER SCHMITZ
DESIGNER:
CHRISTEL TÜRK/
HANS GÜNTER SCHMITZ
AGENCY:
HANS GÜNTER SCHMITZ,
GRUPPE FÜR VISUELLE
KOMMUNIKATION
■ 215

PHOTOGRAPHER:
ERNIE FRIEDLANDER
CLIENT:
APPLE COMPUTER
ART DIRECTOR:
CLEMENT MOK
▼ ■ 216

PHOTOGRAPHER:
LONNIE DUKA
CLIENT:
MCI INTERNATIONAL INC.
ART DIRECTOR:
BILL CORRIDORI
DESIGNER:
BILL CORRIDORI
■ 217

■ 215 A contemporary tile oven designed by Manfred Lang of Pro Industria for Olsberg. (GER)

■ 216 New equipment introductions of Apple Computer in 1987. The photograph, which was used for a catalog, extends over a double spread and two fold-out pages. (USA)

■ 217 From a series of photographs of the MCI telephone company's earth stations. (USA)

■ 215 Ein moderner Kachelofen, entworfen von Manfred Lang von Pro Industria für Olsberg. (GER)

■ 216 Neueinführungen von Apple Computer 1987. Die Aufnahme wurde für einen Katalog verwendet und reicht über eine Doppelseite mit zwei Auslegern. (USA)

■ 217 Aus einer Serie von Aufnahmen der Erdstationen der Telephongesellschaft MCI. (USA)

■ 215 Poêle de faïence de conception moderne créée par Manfred Lang de Pro Industria pour Olsberg. (GER)

■ 216 Photo double page plus deux rabats pour un catalogue des nouveautés Apple 1987. Le constructeur d'ordinateurs y annonce ses nouveaux équipements. (USA)

■ 217 Photo tirée d'une série de vues de stations terriennes de télécommunications des Téléphones MCI. (USA)

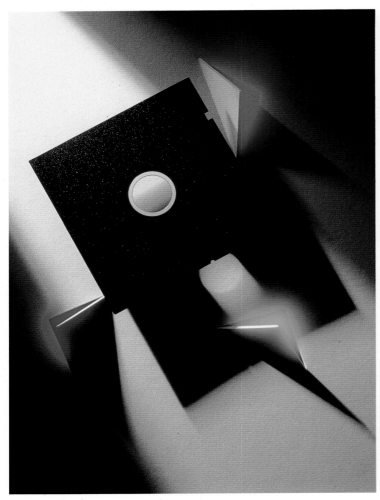

PHOTOGRAPHER:
RICK GAYLE
CLIENT:
HONEYWELL
ART DIRECTOR:
MEG IWATA
DESIGNER:
MEG IWATA
■ 218

PHOTOGRAPHER:
GERALD BYBEE
PUBLISHER:
PARAGON PRESS/
BYBEE STUDIOS
ART DIRECTOR:
GERALD BYBEE/ADRIAN PULFER
DESIGNER:
ADRIAN PULFER/CLIFF MORGAN
■ 219

■ 218 From a series of photographs used for the covers of software brochures for Honeywell. (USA)

■ 219 From a brochure which served as a joint promotion for printer, paper manufacturer, and photographer. (USA)

■ 220 Photograph used in an advertising campaign for *Blaupunkt* products. (NLD)

■ 218 Aus einer Serie von Aufnahmen für Umschläge von Software-Broschüren der Firma Honeywell. (USA)

■ 219 Aus einer Broschüre als Gemeinschaftswerbung für den Drucker, Papierhersteller und Photographen. (USA)

■ 220 In einer Werbekampagne für *Blaupunkt*-Geräte verwendete Aufnahme. (NLD)

■ 218 D'une série de photos utilisée pour des couvertures de brochures sur le «Software» de Honeywell. (USA)

■ 219 Photo utilisée pour une brochure de promotion collective de l'imprimeur, du papetier et du photographe. (USA)

■ 220 Photo utilisée dans une campagne de publicité pour les produits *Blaupunkt*. (NLD)

PHOTOGRAPHER:
MICHAEL STEENMEIJER
CLIENT:
BLAUPUNKT
ART DIRECTOR:
PETER RIGBY/
ROY KAHMANN
AGENCY:
SAATCHI & SAATCHI
■ 220

PHOTOGRAPHER:
DIETMAR HENNEKA
CLIENT:
FROGDESIGN
DESIGNER:
DIETMAR HENNEKA
AGENCY:
FROGDESIGN
■ 221, 222

■ 221, 222 Photographs depicting a *Sony* TV and a telephone by SEL, used in an advertising campaign for industrial design by frogdesign. (GER)

■ 221, 222 Aufnahmen aus einer Werbekampagne für Industrie-Design von frogdesign, hier ein *Sony*-Fernsehgerät und ein SEL-Telephon. (GER)

■ 221, 222 Photos pour une campagne publicitaire du studio d'esthétique industrielle frogdesign, ici un TV *Sony* et un téléphone SEL. (GER)

■ 223, 224 From a brochure introducing a new line of sun glasses. The objective was to call attention to the *Polar Blue Filters* of the *Nautilus* brand and to the high quality of the product. (USA)

■ 225, 226 Fruits and leather. Examples of the photographs for an agenda designed for Lackawanna, a manufacturer of leather products. (USA)

■ 223, 224 Für eine Broschüre, in der eine neue Sonnenbrillenlinie vorgestellt wird. Aufgabe war es, die blauen Gläser *(Polar Blue Filters)* der Marke *Nautilus* und die hohe Qualität der Produkte in den Mittelpunkt zu stellen. (USA)

■ 225, 226 Kombinationen von Früchten und Leder – Beispiele der Aufnahmen für eine Agenda des Lederherstellers Lackawanna. (USA)

■ 223, 224 Pour la brochure de présentation d'une nouvelle gamme de lunettes de soleil. L'accent devait être mis sur les verres bleus *(Polar Blue Filters)* de la marque *Nautilus* et la qualité exceptionnelle de ces produits. (USA)

■ 225, 226 Combinaison de fruits et de cuirs – exemples des photos illustrant un agenda du maroquinier Lackawanna. (USA)

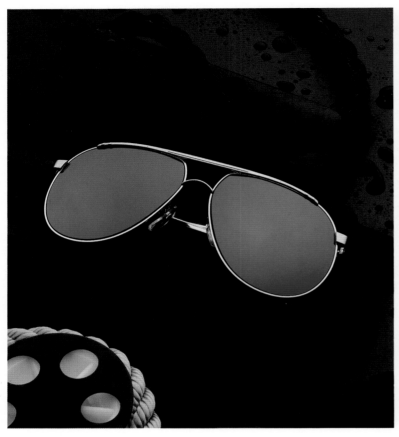

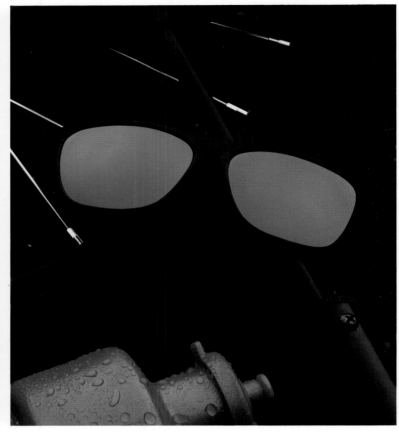

PHOTOGRAPHER:
TOM RYAN
CLIENT:
RENAULD INTERNATIONAL, LTD.
ART DIRECTOR:
GAIL GRIESE
AGENCY:
WOODROW ADVERTISING, INC.
■ 223, 224

PHOTOGRAPHER:
Myron Beck
CLIENT:
Lackawanna Leather Co.
ART DIRECTOR:
Dan Lennon
DESIGNER:
Dan Lennon
AGENCY:
Lennon & Associates
■ 225, 226

PHOTOGRAPHER:
Michael W. Rutherford
CLIENT:
Rutherford Studio
ART DIRECTOR:
Michael W. Rutherford
DESIGNER:
Chuck Creasey
AGENCY:
Chuck Creasey
■ 227, 228

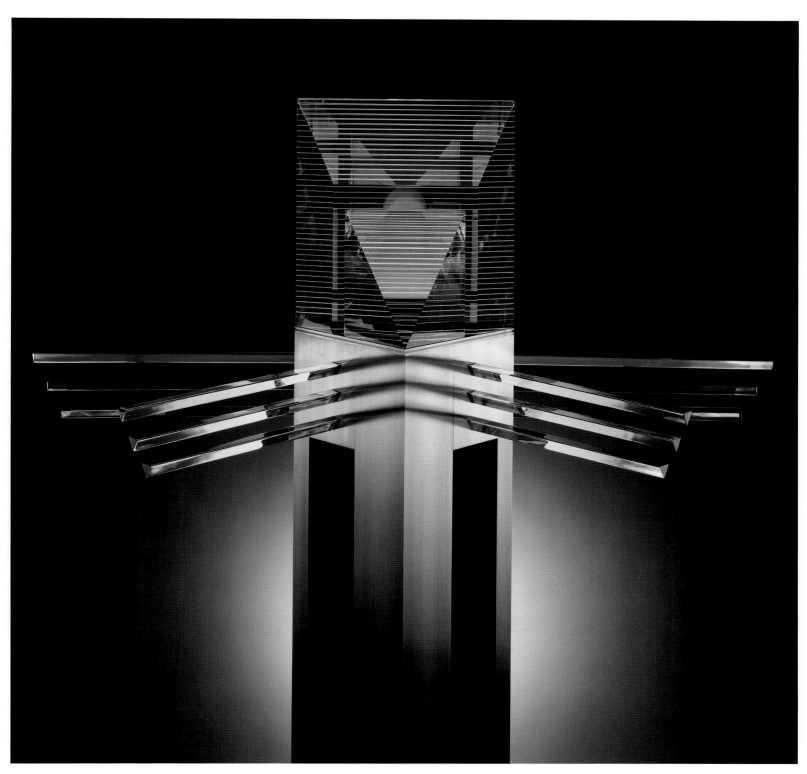

PHOTOGRAPHER:
ROBERT MOORE
CLIENT:
STEUBEN GLASS
ART DIRECTOR:
MARY LOU LITTRELL
DESIGNER:
MARY LOU LITTRELL
■ 229

■ 227, 228 Photographs from a catalog for saddles and bridles of exceptional quality. (USA)

■ 229 From an exhibition catalog entitled "The Steuben Project: Sculptures in Crystal". (USA)

■ 227, 228 Aufnahmen aus einem Katalog für Sattel und Zaumzeug von hochwertiger Qualität. (USA)

■ 229 Aus dem Katalog für eine Ausstellung mit dem Titel «Das Steuben-Projekt: Skulpturen in Kristall». (USA)

■ 227, 228 Photos réalisées pour un catalogue d'équipements d'équitation de grande classe. (USA)

■ 229 Catalogue d'une exposition intitulée «Le projet Steuben: sculptures de cristal». (USA)

PHOTOGRAPHER:
AARON JONES
CLIENT:
NIKE
ART DIRECTOR:
RICK McQUISTON
AGENCY:
WIEDEN & KENNEDY
■ 230

PHOTOGRAPHER:
DANIEL JOUANNEAU
CLIENT:
PARKER
AGENCY:
LOWE HOWARD-SPINK
►■ 231

■ 230 From an eight-page advertising supplement for the *Nike* line of products. (USA)

■ 231 Full-page photograph from an advertisement for *Parker* pens and pencils. Their elegance is compared to that of a 1925 *Hispano Suiza*. (NLD)

■ 230 Aus einer achtseitigen Zeitschriften-Werbebeilage für *Nike*-Produkte. (USA)

■ 231 Ganzseitige Aufnahme aus einer Anzeige für *Parker*-Schreibgeräte, deren Eleganz hier mit der eines *Hispano Suiza* von 1925 verglichen wird. (NLD)

■ 230 Extrait d'un encart publicitaire de magazine de huit pages pour les produits *Nike*. (USA)

■ 231 Photo pleine page pour une annonce de stylos *Parker* dont l'élégance n'est comparable qu'à celle d'un modèle *Hispano Suiza* de 1925. (NLD)

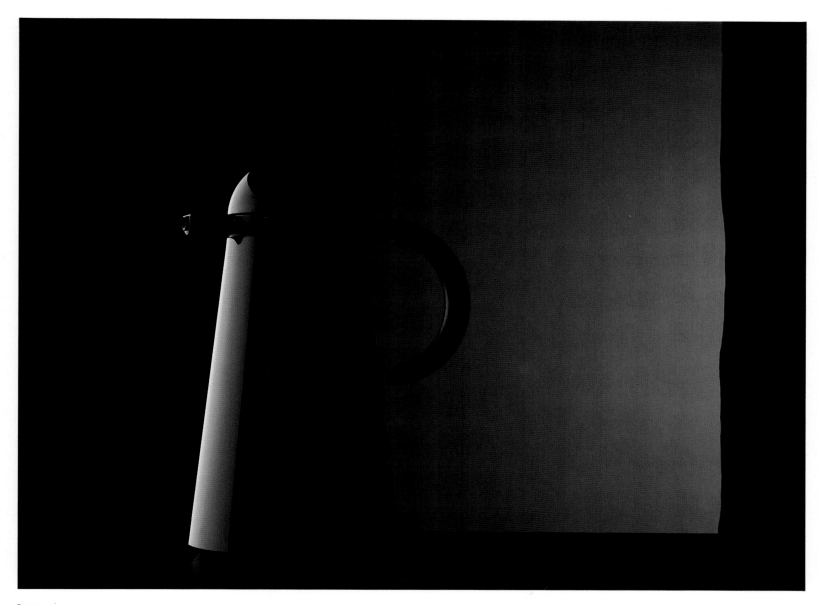

PHOTOGRAPHER:
ULLI WELLINGER/
RAINER HEIDRICH
CLIENT:
ARTSTUDIO
DESIGNER:
ULLI WELLINGER/
RAINER HEIDRICH
◄■ 232

PHOTOGRAPHER:
JOHN PAYNE
ART DIRECTOR:
GEORGE BENSON
DESIGNER:
JOHN PAYNE
■ 233

■ 232 Self-promotion for Artstudio, a team of photographers in Stuttgart. (GER)

■ 233 Photograph used for his own promotion by the Chicago photographer John Payne. (USA)

■ 232 Eigenwerbung eines Photographen-Teams aus Stuttgart, das sich Artstudio nennt. (GER)

■ 233 Als Eigenwerbung verwendete Aufnahme des Photographen John Payne, Chicago. (USA)

■ 232 Autopromotion d'une équipe de photographes constituée en «Artstudio» à Stuttgart. (GER)

■ 233 Photo que son auteur, le photographe John Payne de Chicago, utilise pour sa publicité personnelle. (USA)

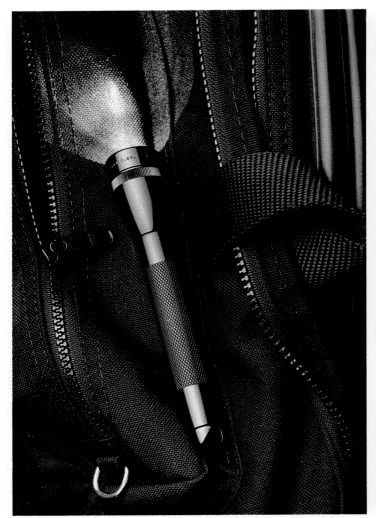

PHOTOGRAPHER:
RICK ENGLISH
CLIENT:
CHIA BEAN, INC.
ART DIRECTOR:
PATRICIA HOLLAND
AGENCY:
THE HOLLAND/ENGLISH GROUP
■ 234

PHOTOGRAPHER:
BILL WHITE
■ 235

■ 234 This photo for Chia Bean, Inc., was designed as an ultimate black-and-white shot with the light from the flashlight providing the visual kick. (USA)

■ 235 Unpublished photograph used as self-promotion by Bill White, New York. (USA)

■ 234 Bei dieser als Schwarzweissbild konzipierten Aufnahme für Chia Bean, Inc., wurde der Lichtstrahl der Taschenlampe als besonderer visueller Reiz eingesetzt. (USA)

■ 235 Unveröffentlichte Aufnahme als Eigenwerbung von Bill White, New York. (USA)

■ 234 Sur cette photo, noir et blanc, créée pour Chia Bean, Inc., le rayon de lumière émanant de la lampe de poche est employé comme effet spécial attirant le regard. (USA)

■ 235 Photo inédite pour l'autopromotion de Bill White de New York. (USA)

SPORT

SPORT

■ 236 "Balance" is the theme of this photograph shown in the photographer's advertising diary. (USA)

■ 237 Photograph used for the Barron Hilton Soaring Cup 1988/1989. (USA)

■ 236 «Gleichgewicht» ist das Thema dieser Aufnahme, die in einer Werbe-Agenda des Photographen gezeigt wird. (USA)

■ 237 Für den «Barron Hilton Segelflug-Cup 1988/1989» verwendete Aufnahme. (USA)

■ 236 «Equilibre», voilà le thème de ce cliché illustrant l'agenda publicitaire d'un photographe. (USA)

■ 237 Photo utilisée pour la Coupe de vol à voile Barron Hilton 1988/1989. (USA)

PHOTOGRAPHER:
JOHN MCDERMOTT
CLIENT:
JOHN MCDERMOTT
ART DIRECTOR:
DIANA GRAHAM
DESIGNER:
DEBRA THOMPSON/WING CHAN
AGENCY:
*DIAGRAM DESIGN AND
MARKETING COMMUNICATIONS*
◄■ 236

PHOTOGRAPHER:
KEVIN CRUFF
CLIENT:
HILTON HOTELS
ART DIRECTOR:
*FORREST AND VALERIE
RICHARDSON*
DESIGNER:
*FORREST AND VALERIE
RICHARDSON*
AGENCY:
RICHARDSON OR RICHARDSON
■ 237

PHOTOGRAPHER:
BERNARD ASSET/
AGENCE VANDYSTADT
PUBLISHER:
ZOOM
ART DIRECTOR:
JOËL LAROCHE
■ 238

■ 238 At the Grand Prix de Monaco 1980 Dekek Daly (Ireland) on Tyrrell is carried from the curve of Sainte Dévote. Published by *Zoom* magazine. (FRA)

■ 239 Sporting events from 1987 were reviewed in pictures in *Sports Illustrated:* shown here is a photo from a rally in Kenya with two Masai tribesmen. (USA)

■ 238 Beim Grossen Preis von Monaco 80 entstandene Aufnahme: Dekek Daly (Irland) auf Tyrrell wird hier aus der Kurve von Sainte Dévote getragen. Aus *Zoom.* (FRA)

■ 239 Ein Sportereignis aus dem Jahre 1987, veröffentlicht in der Zeitschrift *Sports Illustrated:* eine Rallye in Kenia und zwei Angehörige des Masai-Stammes. (USA)

■ 238 Photo réalisée lors du Grand Prix de Monaco 1980. On y voit l'Irlandais Dekek Daly sur Tyrrell quitter la piste dans le virage de Sainte Dévote. Extrait du magazine *Zoom.* (FRA)

■ 239 Manifestation sportive de l'année 1987, illustrée dans le magazine *Sports Illustrated:* rallye automobile au Kenya; deux Masais fournissent la couleur locale. (USA)

Photographer:
Reinhard Klein/SIPA
Publisher:
Time Inc.
Art Director:
Steven Hoffman
Designer:
Steven Hoffman/
Peter Herbert
■ 239

PHOTOGRAPHER:
BERND GRUNDMANN
DESIGNER:
BERND GRUNDMANN
■ 240

■ 240 Unpublished shot
taken by photographer
Bernd Grundmann. (SWI)

■ 240 Unveröffentlichte Aufnahme des Photographen
Bernd Grundmann. (SWI)

■ 240 Photo inédite réalisée
par les soins du photographe
Bernd Grundmann. (SWI)

JOURNALISM

JOURNALISME

JOURNALISMUS

JOURNALISME

PHOTOGRAPHER:
Joel C. Freid
CLIENT:
Joel Freid Photography, Inc.
ART DIRECTOR:
Jack Beveridge
DESIGNER:
Jack Beveridge
AGENCY:
Beveridge Byrd & Seay
■ 241–244

PHOTOGRAPHER:
David Turnley/BLACK STAR
PUBLISHER:
Gruner + Jahr AG & Co.
ART DIRECTOR:
Erwin Ehret
■ 245

■ 241-244 Pictures of a journey through Eastern Europe. "Baggage Woman", "Radiator Boy", and "Suceava North" were taken in Suceava, Rumania. *244* "Early Morning" was taken in Krakow, Poland. (USA)

■ 245 A scene from South Africa. A white pupil from an English private school boards the same train, but not the same compartment, as the black household servants. From an article in *Geo.* (GER)

■ 241-244 Bilder einer Reise durch Osteuropa: «Gepäck-frau», «Heizungsjunge», «Suceava Nord», alle in Suceava, Rumänien, aufgenommen. *244:* «Früher Morgen», Krakau, Polen. (USA)

■ 245 Eine Szene aus Südafrika: ein weisser Schüler einer englischen Privatschule, der mit den schwarzen Hausange-stellten zwar in einen Zug, aber nicht in dasselbe Abteil steigen wird. Aus einem Beitrag in *Geo.* (GER)

■ 241-244 Images d'un voyage en Europe de l'Est: «baga-giste», «préposé au chauffage», «Suceava Nord» – 3 photos de Suceava, en Roumanie. *244:* «Tôt le matin», Cracovie, Pologne. (USA)

■ 245 Scène d'Afrique du Sud: écolier blanc d'une école privée anglaise qui va monter dans le même train, mais pas dans le même compartiment que les domestiques noirs. Tiré d'un reportage du magazine *Geo.* (GER)

PHOTOGRAPHER:
JAMES NACHTWEY/MAGNUM
PUBLISHER:
EASTMAN KODAK COMPANY
ART DIRECTOR:
KAI MUI
AGENCY:
RUMRILL-HOYT, INC.
■ 246

■ 246 "Point Blank", photograph taken by a photojournalist for use by Kodak in an advertising campaign for *Kodak Professional Film.* (USA)

■ 247, 248 From a report on Managua published in *Life.* It shows two young men who were drafted into the war when they were 17 and who were discharged as invalids, and veterans who are members of the present government and who are decorating each other with medals. (USA)

■ 246 «Point Blank», Aufnahme eines Photojournalisten, die von Kodak für eine Werbekampagne für *Kodak Professional Film* verwendet wurde. (USA)

■ 247, 248 Aus einem Bericht über Managua in der Zeitschrift *Life:* Zwei junge Männer, die, mit 17 eingezogen, als Invalide aus dem Krieg zurückkehren, und Veteranen, die heute Regierungsposten innehaben und sich gegenseitig mit Medaillen der Revolution auszeichnen. (USA)

■ 246 «Point Blank», par un reporter photo – cliché utilisé par Kodak pour une campagne de presse en faveur du *Kodak Professional Film.* (USA)

■ 247, 248 Reportage du magazine *Life* sur Managua: deux jeunes gens mobilisés à 17 ans reviennent invalides de la guerre; des vétéranes aujourd'hui promus à des postes gouvernementaux se décernent mutuellement des médailles révolutionnaires. (USA)

PHOTOGRAPHER:
Diego Goldberg/SYGMA
PUBLISHER:
Time, Inc.
ART DIRECTOR:
Tom Bentkowski
DESIGNER:
Tom Bentkowski
■ 247, 248

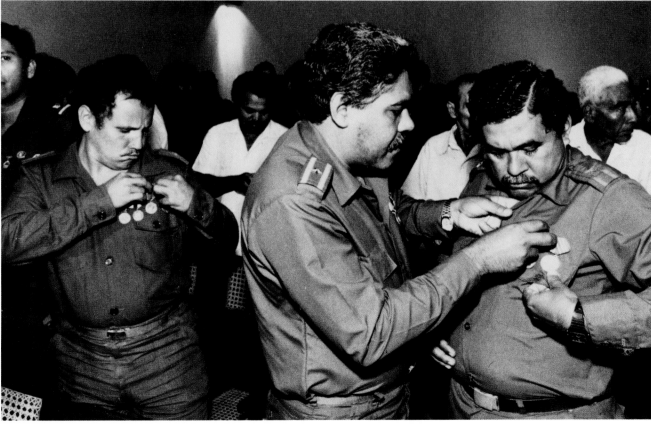

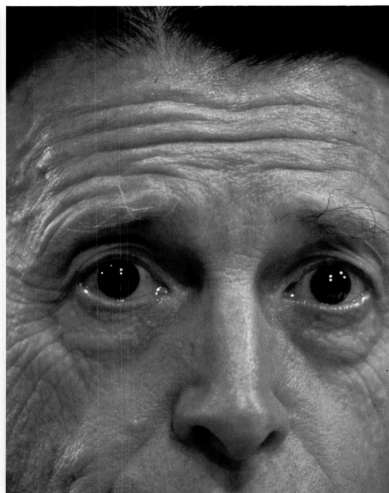

PHOTOGRAPHER:
ENRICO FERORELLI
PUBLISHER:
TIME, INC.
ART DIRECTOR:
TOM BENTKOWSKI
DESIGNER:
TOM BENTKOWSKI
■ 249–251

■ 249–251 George Schultz, Caspar Weinberger, and Oliver North. Two full-page photographs and a double-spread portrait from a report on the Iran Contra hearings in the United States as published in *Life*. (USA)

■ 252 Oliver North taking the oath during the Iran Contra hearings. From an article published in *Time*. (USA)

■ 249–251 George Schultz, Caspar Weinberger und Oliver North: zwei ganzseitige Aufnahmen und ein doppelseitiges Portrait aus einem Bildbericht über die Iran-Contra-Hearings in den USA, veröffentlicht in *Life*. (USA)

■ 252 Oliver North beim Ablegen des Eides während der Iran-Contra-Hearings, aus einem Artikel in *Time*. (USA)

■ 249–251 George Schultz, Caspar Weinberger et Oliver North: deux photos pleine page et un portrait double page illustrent un reportage sur l'enquête sénatoriale de l'Irangate aux Etats-Unis publié dans *Life*. (USA)

■ 252 Oliver North lors de sa prestation de serment devant la commission d'enquête sur l'Irangate, dans *Time*. (USA)

Photographer:
Terry Ashe
Publisher:
Time, Inc.
Art Director:
Rudy Hoglund
Designer:
Nigel Holmes
■ 252

PHOTOGRAPHER:
MARY ELLEN MARK
PUBLISHER:
TIME, INC.
ART DIRECTOR:
CHARLES W. PATES
DESIGNER:
NORA SHEEHAN
■ 253

PHOTOGRAPHER:
GEOFFREY CLIFFORD
PUBLISHER:
TIME, INC.
ART DIRECTOR:
TOM BENTKOWSKI
DESIGNER:
TOM BENTKOWSKI
► ■ 254

■ 253 Photograph taken for an article published in *Life* entitled "Child of Silence". Retrieved from the shadow world of autism, Katy finds her voice. (USA)

■ 254 "At Home in Vietnam". The photograph from this report was taken at the conservatory in Hanoi. Eastern European folk music being played on an accordion is an indication of Vietnam's opening to the West. Published in *Life*. (USA)

■ 253 «Kind des Schweigens» ist der Titel des Artikels über ein autistisches Mädchen, das dank einer Therapie seine Stimme findet. Aus *Life*. (USA)

■ 254 Aus einem Bericht über «Vietnam heute» in der Zeitschrift *Life*. Hier eine Aufnahme aus dem Konservatorium in Hanoi: Ein Akkordeonspieler, der osteuropäische Volksmusik spielt – ein Zeichen für Vietnams Öffnung nach Westen. (USA)

■ 253 «L'Enfant du silence», tel est le titre de l'article illustré par cette photo d'une enfant autiste qui retrouve sa voix en cours de traitement. Magazine *Life*. (USA)

■ 254 Photo pour un reportage du magazine *Life* sur «le Viêt-nam aujourd'hui». On voit ici une scène au conservatoire de Hanoi: un accordéoniste joue de la musique populaire de l'Est de l'Europe, signe de l'ouverture politique du pays. (USA)

PHOTOGRAPHER:
ANTHONY SUAU/BLACK STAR
PUBLISHER:
FILIPACCHI
ART DIRECTOR:
ERIC COLMET DAAGE
■ 255

■ 255 From an article in *Photo* on the photographer Anthony Suau, Pulitzer Prize winner at age 26. The picture shows a girl in Lérida, Columbia, who was saved after being trapped for 36 hours in mud slides. (FRA)

■ 256 South Korean police with riot shields during a demonstration in Masan in 1987. From *Stern*. (GER)

■ 257 "Lebanon, Armenians in Anjar". Photograph used by Wolfgang Kunz for his own promotion. (GER)

■ 255 Aus einem Artikel in *Photo* über den Photographen Anthony Suau, der mit 26 Jahren den Pulitzer-Preis erhielt. Lérida, Kolumbien: ein Mädchen, das nach 36 Stunden aus den Schlammassen gerettet wurde. (FRA)

■ 256 Südkoreanische Polizei mit Schutzschildern bei einer Demonstration in Masan, 1987. Aus dem *Stern*. (GER)

■ 257 «Libanon, Armenier in Anjar». Eigenwerbung des Photographen Wolfgang Kunz. (GER)

■ 255 Illustration d'un article que *Photo* consacre au photographe Anthony Suau, lauréat du prix Pulitzer à 26 ans: photo d'une rescapée sauvée après avoir été prisonnière de la boue pendant 36 heures à Lérida, en Colombie. (FRA)

■ 256 Police sud-coréenne armée de boucliers lors d'une manifestation à Masan en 1987. Magazine *Stern*. (GER)

■ 257 «Liban, Arméniens d'Anjar.» Photo autopromotionnelle du photographe Wolfgang Kunz. (GER)

PHOTOGRAPHER:
CHARLIE COLE/PICTURE GROUP
PUBLISHER:
GRUNER + JAHR AG & CO.
AGENCY:
PICTURE GROUP INC.
■ 256

PHOTOGRAPHER:
WOLFGANG KUNZ/BILDERBERG
■ 257

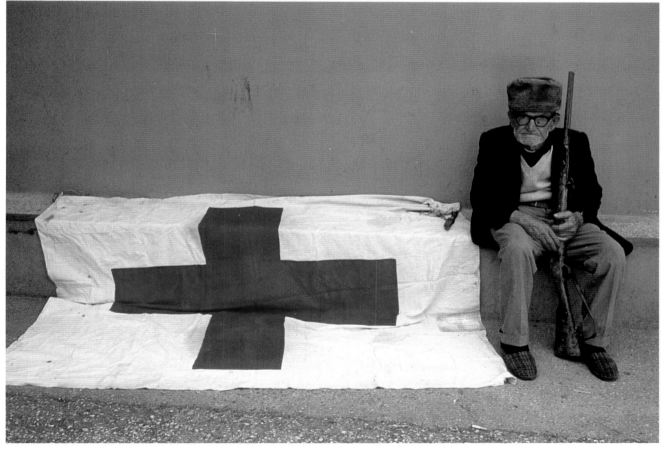

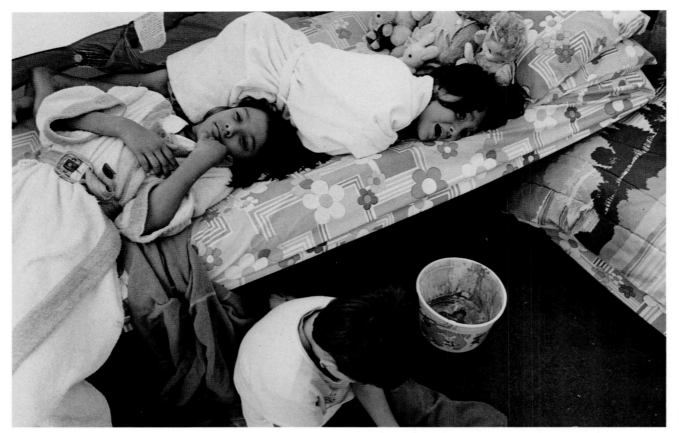

PHOTOGRAPHER:
STEPHENIE HOLLYMAN
PUBLISHER:
PHILOSOPHICAL LIBRARY
DESIGNER:
MICHAEL BIERUT
AGENCY:
VIGNELLI ASSOCIATES
■ 258–261

■ 258–261 From a pictorial volume by the photo journalist Stephenie Hollyman entitled *We the Homeless* and published by the Philosophical Library Inc. The black-and-white photographs portray America's displaced and vagrant people. (USA)

■ 258–261 Aus einem Bildband der Photojournalistin Stephenie Hollyman, der unter dem Titel *We The Homeless* (Wir, die Heimatlosen) bei Philosophical Library Inc. erschienen ist. Es sind Schwarzweissaufnahmen von Obdachlosen in den USA. (USA)

■ 258–261 Illustrations pour l'album de la journaliste photo Stephenie Hollyman intitulé *We The Homeless* (Nous les Sans-abri), paru aux Editions Philosophical Library Inc. Photos noir et blanc des sans-logis d'Amérique. (USA)

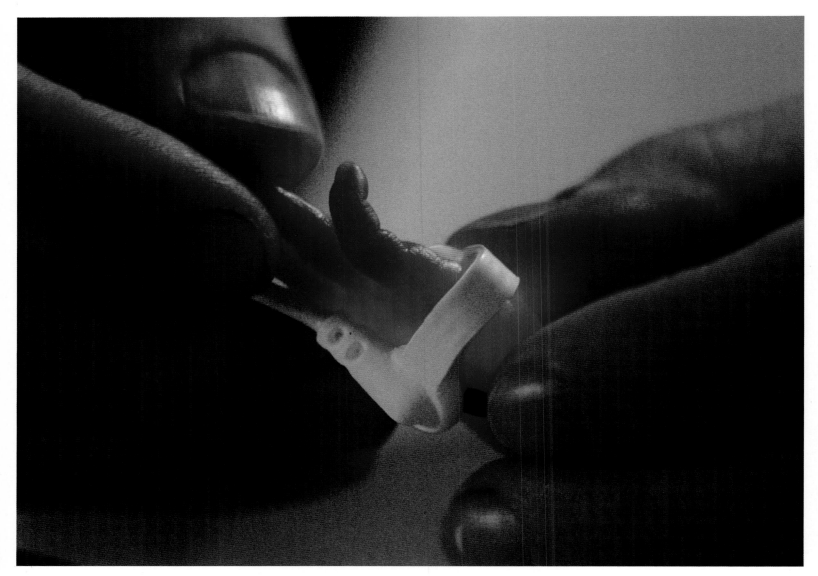

PHOTOGRAPHER:
THOMAS STEPHAN
PUBLISHER:
GRUNER + JAHR AG & CO.
ART DIRECTOR:
ERWIN EHRET
■ 262

■ 262 Photograph of the tiny hand of a prematurely-born baby, and the head of an instrument which continuously measures the current oxygen content of the blood by determining the absorption of red and infrared wavelengths. From a report in *Geo* about a doctor's struggle to save the lives of quintuplets who were born three months prematurely. (GER)

■ 262 Die winzige Hand eines extrem unreif geborenen Kindes, mit dem Messkopf eines Instrumentes, das aus der Absorption von rotem und infrarotem Licht fortwährend den aktuellen Sauerstoffgehalt des Blutes errechnet. Aufnahme aus einem Artikel in *Geo,* in dem ein Arzt über den Kampf um das Leben von Fünflingen berichtet, die drei Monate zu früh zur Welt kamen. (GER)

■ 262 La main minuscle d'un prématuré, avec la tête de mesure d'un instrument indiquant en continu la teneur du sang en oxygène sur la base de l'absorption de lumière rouge et infrarouge. Photo pour un article de *Geo* où un médecin narre le combat mené pour maintenir en vie des quintuplés venus au monde trois mois trop tôt, et la somme d'efforts investie dans cette aventure. (GER)

STILL LIFE

NATURE MORTE

STILLEBEN

PHOTOGRAPHER:
Kathryn Kleinman
STYLIST:
Sara Slavin
PUBLISHER:
Chronicle Books
ART DIRECTOR:
Kathryn Kleinman/
Sara Slavin
DESIGNER:
Michael Mabry
■ 263

PHOTOGRAPHER:
Chuck Shotwell
CLIENT:
Shotwell & Associates
ART DIRECTOR:
Steve Liska
DESIGNER:
Beth Karnes
AGENCY:
Liska & Associates
► ■ 264

■ 263 Sample photo taken from a book of photographs by Kathryn Kleinman, entitled *On Flowers* and published by Chronical Books. (USA)

■ 264 Shot used for self-promotional purposes, taken by photographer Chuck Shotwell. (USA)

■ 263 Aufnahme aus einem Bildband der Photographin Kathryn Kleinman mit dem Titel *On Flowers*, erschienen bei Chronical Books. (USA)

■ 264 Als Eigenwerbung des Photographen Chuck Shotwell verwendete Aufnahme. (USA)

■ 263 Photo tirée d'un album de la photographe Kathryn Kleinman intitulé *On Flowers* (Des Fleurs) et paru aux Editions Chronical Books. (USA)

■ 264 Photo que le photographe Chuck Shotwell utilise pour sa publicité personnelle. (USA)

PHOTOGRAPHER:
PHILIP BEKKER
ART DIRECTOR:
PHILIP BEKKER
DESIGNER:
PHILIP BEKKER
STUDIO:
PHILIP BEKKER PHOTOGRAPHY
■ 265-267

■ 265-267 Personal studies by photographer Philip Bekker. Shown: two examples from his "Pepper" series, and an example from a series using skull and red objects. (USA)

■ 265-267 Persönliche Studien des Photographen Philip Bekker: Beispiele aus einer Serie mit Paprikaschoten und aus einer Serie mit Schädel und roten Objekten. (USA)

■ 265-267 Études personnelles du photographe Philip Bekker: exemples d'une série de gousses de paprika, et d'une série utilisant un crâne et des objets rouges. (USA)

PHOTOGRAPHER:
MICHAEL GEIGER
PUBLISHER:
FOTOFOLIO
■ 268-270

■268-270 Examples from a still life with flowers series, also available on general sale as postcards. (USA)

■268-270 Beispiele aus einer Serie von Stilleben mit Blumen, die auch als Postkarten erhältlich sind. (USA)

■268-270 Exemples tirés d'une série de natures mortes aux fleurs également reproduite sur cartes postales. (USA)

■ 271–274 Shots from a still life flower series by photographer Michael Geiger, published by Fotofolio. (USA)

■ 271–274 Für eine bei Fotofolio erschienene Kartenreihe mit Blumenstilleben des Photographen Michael Geiger. (USA)

■ 271–274 Pour une série de cartes des Editions Fotofolio: natures mortes aux fleurs par Michael Geiger. (USA)

PHOTOGRAPHER:
MICHAEL GEIGER
PUBLISHER:
FOTOFOLIO
■ 271–274

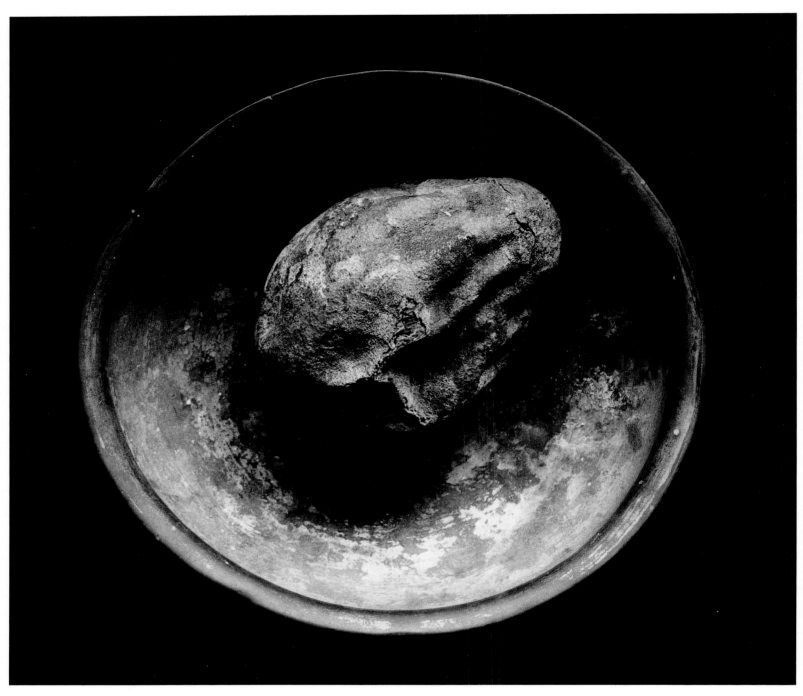

PHOTOGRAPHER:
ANATOLY PRONIN
■ 275, 276

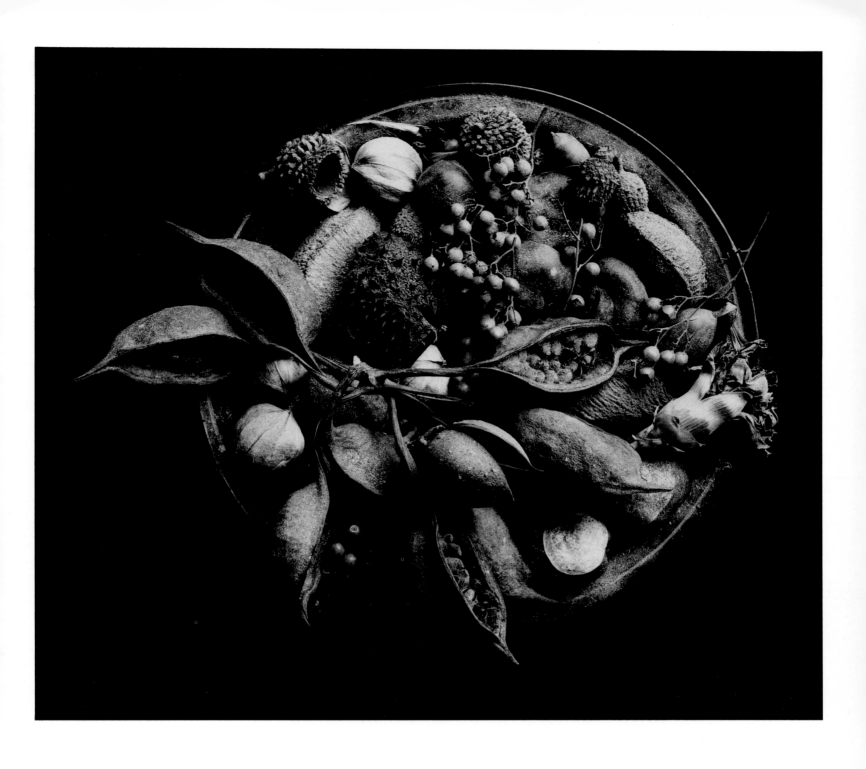

■ 275, 276 Still life in black and white; shots used as self-promotion by photographer Anatoly Pronin. (USA)

■ 275, 276 Stilleben in Schwarzweiss; als Eigenwerbung des Photographen Anatoly Pronin verwendet. (USA)

■ 275, 276 Natures mortes en noir et blanc. Photos auto-promotionnelles du photographe Anatoly Pronin. (USA)

PHOTOGRAPHER:
DAVID STEWART
CLIENT:
MICHAEL PETERS LITERATURE
ART DIRECTOR:
DAVID STOCKS
◄■ 279

PHOTOGRAPHER:
DAVID STEWART
■ 277, 278

■ 277, 278 From a series of still lifes, taken by London photographer David Stewart and used as self-promotion. (GBR)

■ 279 Photograph used for an annual report of the Michael Peters Group. (GBR)

■ 277, 278 Aufnahmen des Londoner Photographen David Stewart, die er als Eigenwerbung verwendet hat. (GBR)

■ 279 Aufnahme für einen Jahresbericht der Michael-Peters-Gruppe. (GBR)

■ 277, 278 D'une série de photos que le photographe David Stewart, Londres, utilise pour sa publicité personnelle. (GBR)

■ 279 Photo utilisée pour un rapport annuel du Michael Peters Group. (GBR)

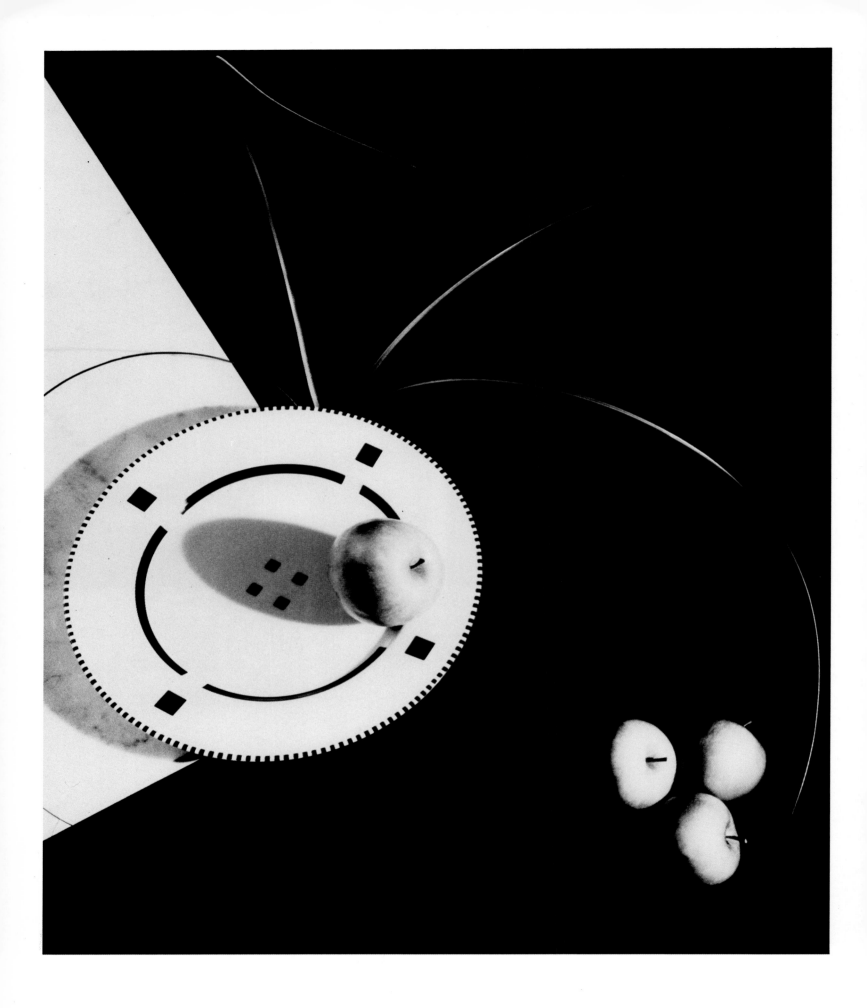

PHOTOGRAPHER:
LAURENCE BACH
CLIENT:
CITICORP
ART DIRECTOR:
ROBERT WARKULWIZ/
MICHAEL ROGALSKI/
WILLIAM F. SMITH
DESIGNER:
ROBERT J. WARKULWIZ/
MICHAEL ROGALSKI/
WILLIAM F. SMITH
AGENCY:
WARKULWIZ DESIGN ASSOCIATES
◄ ■ 280

PHOTOGRAPHER:
GRANT PETERSON
STYLIST:
ALECIA BELDEGREEN
PUBLISHER:
EASTMAN KODAK COMPANY
ART DIRECTOR:
STEPHEN HALL
AGENCY:
RUMRILL-HOYT, INC.
■ 281

■ 280 Black-and-white photograph entitled "Choice" taken from a Citicorp brochure: "The Stock Purchase Plan gives you more than one choice." (USA)

■ 281 Photograph taken by New Yorker Grant Peterson and used for *Kodak* advertising. (USA)

■ 280 Aufnahme aus einer Broschüre von Citicorp. Es geht hier um verschiedene Entscheidungsmöglichkeiten beim Kauf von Aktien. Der Titel der Aufnahme: Auswahl. (USA)

■ 281 Für *Kodak*-Werbung verwendete Aufnahme des New Yorker Photographen Grant Peterson. (USA)

■ 280 Photo noir et blanc illustrant une brochure de Citicorp. Il s'agit ici des diverses décisions possibles lors de l'achat d'actions, d'où le titre «Choix». (USA)

■ 281 Photo réalisée par le photographe new-yorkais Grant Peterson pour la promotion *Kodak*. (USA)

PHOTOGRAPHER:
Ken Matsubara
STYLIST:
Ken Matsubara
PUBLISHER:
Zoom
ART DIRECTOR:
Joël Laroche
■ 282, 283

■ 282, 283 From an article in *Zoom* photo magazine about Ken Matsubara to coincide with an exhibition of his photographs in a Parisian gallery. The photographer took these shots with a special camera (20 x 24 inch) in the New York Polaroid Studio. (USA)

■ 282, 283 Aus einem Artikel im Photomagazin *Zoom* über Ken Matsubara anlässlich einer Ausstellung seiner Photos in einer Pariser Galerie. Diese Aufnahmen machte der Photograph mit einer Spezial-Kamera (20 x 24 inch) im New Yorker Polaroid-Studio. (USA)

■ 282, 283 Photos tirées d'un article du magazine photo *Zoom* à l'occasion d'une exposition des photos de Ken Matsubara dans une galerie parisienne. L'artiste les a réalisées à l'aide d'un appareil spécial de 20 x 24 pouces au studio new-yorkais de Polaroïd. (USA)

PHOTOGRAPHER:
Sinan Koçaslan
STUDIO:
Tanitim Laboratuari Ltd.
■ 284

PHOTOGRAPHER:
Scott Van Sicklin
ART DIRECTOR:
Scott Van Sicklin
DESIGNER:
Scott Van Sicklin
■ 285

PHOTOGRAPHER:
Kenro Izu
PUBLISHER:
Eastman Kodak Company
ART DIRECTOR:
Stephen Hall
AGENCY:
Rumrill-Hoyt, Inc.
►■ 286

■ 284 Shot used for self-promotional purposes, taken by the Turkish photographer Sinan Koçaslan. (TUR)

■ 285 Personal study from an ongoing series by Scott Van Sicklin with found objects from man and nature. (USA)

■ 286 Photograph from *Photography International* magazine issued by Kodak, in which photographers who work with *Kodak Professional Film* are presented. This example, shot by Kenro Izu, belongs to a series of personal studies with flowers. (USA)

■ 284 Als Eigenwerbung verwendete Aufnahme des türkischen Photographen Sinan Koçaslan. (TUR)

■ 285 Persönliche Studie des Photographen Scott Van Sicklin aus einer Serie mit «Objets trouvés». (USA)

■ 286 Aufnahme aus dem von Kodak herausgegebenen Magazin *Photography International*, in dem Photographen vorgestellt werden, die mit *Kodak Professional Film* arbeiten. Dieses Beispiel gehört zu einer Reihe persönlicher Studien mit Blumen von Kenro Izu. (USA)

■ 284 Cette photo réalisée par le photographe turc Sinan Koçaslan lui sert d'autopromotion. (TUR)

■ 285 Étude personnelle d'une série de Scott Van Sicklin, avec objets trouvés – de l'homme et de la nature. (USA)

■ 286 Photo parue dans le magazine *Photography International* de Kodak en compagnie d'autres créations d'artistes travaillant avec le même film *Kodak Professional Film*. L'exemple montré ici fait partie d'une série d'études personnelles de fleurs par Kenro Izu. (USA)

■ 287 From a four-part series presenting the "environment" of photo agency DeAnn Delbridge, San Francisco. (USA)

■ 288 Photograph used for *Macintosh* software. (USA)

■ 287 Aus einer vierteiligen Serie, die das «Umfeld» der Photoagentur DeAnn Delbridge, darstellt. (USA)

■ 288 Aufnahme für *Macintosh*-Software. (USA)

■ 287 D'une série montrant l'«environnement» de l'agence DeAnn Delbridge de San Francisco. (USA)

■ 288 Photo utilisée pour les logiciels *Macintosh*. (USA)

PHOTOGRAPHER:
RICK ENGLISH
◄ ■ 287

PHOTOGRAPHER:
RICK ENGLISH
CLIENT:
PARACOMP INC.
ART DIRECTOR:
BILL ROLLINSON
DESIGNER:
LAURA BAUER
AGENCY:
ROLLINSON DESIGN
■ 288

PHOTOGRAPHER:
TERRY HEFFERNAN
CLIENT:
AMERICAN PRESIDENT LINES
DESIGNER:
KIT HINRICHS
AGENCY:
PENTAGRAM
■ 289, 290

PHOTOGRAPHER:
TERRY HEFFERNAN
CLIENT:
*WEYERHAEUSER PAPER
COMPANY*
ART DIRECTOR:
JOHN VAN DYKE
DESIGNER:
JOHN VAN DYKE
AGENCY:
VAN DYKE COMPANY
■ 291-293

■ 289, 290 From a diary issued by American President Lines. The shots relate to the Pacific mail service introduced in 1917 with the direct route Manila, Singapore, Calcutta, and Ceylon, and to the new steamship network brought about by the Californian goldrush in 1849. (USA)

■ 291-293 Photographs from an annual report for Weyerhaeuser, the paper and cartonage manufacturers. Various customers of the company are presented. (USA)

■ 289, 290 Aus einer Agenda für American President Lines. Hier geht es um die Einführung des Pazifik-Postdienstes 1917 mit einer direkten Route Manila, Singapur, Kalkutta, Ceylon und den durch das Goldfieber in Kalifornien 1849 bedingten neuen Dampfschiffeinsatz. (USA)

■ 291-293 Aufnahmen aus einem Jahresbericht des Papier- und Kartonageherstellers Weyerhaeuser. Es werden verschiedene Kunden der Firma vorgestellt. (USA)

■ 289, 290 Pour un agenda d'American President Lines. Il s'agit ici du lancement du service de courrier pacifique en 1917 sur la route Manille-Singapour-Calcutta-Ceylan et de la mise en service de nouveaux vapeurs à destination de la Californie dès la ruée vers l'or de 1849. (USA)

■ 291-293 Photos pour un rapport annuel du fabricant de papiers et cartonnages Weyerhaeuser. On y présente divers clients de l'entreprise. (USA)

PHOTOGRAPHER:
KEVIN LA TONA
STYLIST:
SYLVIA SOUTH
DESIGNER:
SYLVIA SOUTH
STUDIO:
LA TONA PRODUCTIONS
■ 294, 295

PHOTOGRAPHER:
GRANT PETERSON
STYLIST:
DONNA FERRARI
PUBLISHER:
CONDÉ NAST PUBLICATIONS
ART DIRECTOR:
PHYLLIS COX
DESIGNER:
BETTY SARONSON
STUDIO:
BRIDE'S
► ■ 296

■ 294, 295 Examples from an ongoing direct-mail campaign for the photography of Kevin LaTona and Sylvia South of Seattle. (USA)

■ 296 Shot accompanying an article about the effect of colors in everyday life, such as the color green, in *Bride's* magazine. (USA)

■ 294, 295 Beispiele aus einer Direct-Mail-Werbekampagne für die Aufnahmen des Teams Kevin LaTona und Sylvia South aus Seattle. (USA)

■ 296 Aufnahme aus einem Artikel in der Zeitschrift *Bride's* über die Wirkung von Farben im täglichen Umgang, wie z.B. Grün. (USA)

■ 294, 295 Exemples figurant dans une campagne de publicité directe pour la photographie de l'équipe Kevin LaTona et Sylvia South de Seattle. (USA)

■ 296 Pour un article interprétant la signification des couleurs dans la vie quotidienne dans le magazine *Bride's* – ici les vertus du vert dans le ménage. (USA)

PHOTOGRAPHER:
POUL IB HENRIKSEN
PUBLISHER:
ECCO SHOES
ART DIRECTOR:
POUL IB HENRIKSEN
DESIGNER:
POUL IB HENRIKSEN
STUDIO:
POUL IB HENRIKSEN
◀■ 297

PHOTOGRAPHER:
AARON JONES
ART DIRECTOR:
AARON JONES
■ 298

■ 297 Photograph used as illustration in an anniversary book issued by *Ecco* shoes. The theme: "Visions of the Future". (DEN)

■ 298 Variation on a theme: Still life with colored light, shot by Aaron Jones. (USA)

■ 297 Als Illustration in einem Jubiläums-Buch von *Ecco*-Schuhen verwendete Aufnahme. Das Thema: «Zukunfts-visionen». (DEN)

■ 298 Variation eines Themas: Stilleben mit farbigem Licht, von Aaron Jones. (USA)

■ 297 Une des photos utilisées pour l'illustration d'un ouvrage commémoratif du chausseur *Ecco*. Le thème: «Visions d'avenir». (DEN)

■ 298 Variation sur le sujet des natures mortes aux effets lumineux, par Aaron Jones. (USA)

PHOTOGRAPHER:
GRANT PETERSON
STYLIST:
DONNA FERRARI
PUBLISHER:
CONDÉ NAST
PUBLICATIONS INC.
ART DIRECTOR:
PHYLLIS COX
DESIGNER:
BETTY SARONSON
STUDIO:
BRIDE'S
■ 299, 301

PHOTOGRAPHER:
GRANT PETERSON
STYLIST:
MAURA MCEVOY
PUBLISHER:
THE HEARST CORPORATION
ART DIRECTOR:
SANDRA DIPASQUA
STUDIO:
CONNOISSEUR
■ 300

■ 299, 301 Photographs published in *Bride's.* (USA)

■ 300 For an article in *Connoisseur* magazine. (USA)

■ 299, 301 Aufnahmen aus der Zeitschrift *Bride's.* (USA)

■ 300 Für einen Artikel im Magazin *Connoisseur.* (USA)

■ 299, 301 Photos tirées du magazine *Bride's.* (USA)

■ 300 Pour un article dans le magazine *Connoisseur.* (USA)

PHOTOGRAPHER:
PAUL FRANZ-MOORE
CLIENT:
FRANZ-MOORE STUDIO
ART DIRECTOR:
PAUL FRANZ-MOORE
STUDIO:
FRANZ-MOORE STUDIO
■ 302, 303

■ 302, 303 From a series of photographs with the title "Offerings", by Paul Franz-Moore. *302:* "Homage to Uncle Floyd." (USA)

■ 302, 303 Beispiele aus einer Serie von Aufnahmen mit dem Titel «Offerings» (Gaben) von Paul Franz-Moore. *302:* «Hommage an Onkel Floyd.» (USA)

■ 302, 303 Photos tirées de la série «Offerings» (Présents) de Paul Franz-Moore. *302:* «Hommage à l'oncle Floyd.» (USA)

PHOTOGRAPHER:
Chuck Shotwell
CLIENT:
Shotwell & Associates
ART DIRECTOR:
Steve Liska
DESIGNER:
Beth Karnes
AGENCY:
Liska & Associates
■ 304

■ 304 This photograph was taken by photographer Chuck Shotwell for a self-promotional poster. (USA)

■ 305 Self-promotional shot by Sicco Kolff. (NLD)

■ 304 Für ein Eigenwerbungsplakat des Photographen Chuck Shotwell verwendete Aufnahme. (USA)

■ 305 Eigenwerbung des Photographen Sicco Kolff. (NLD)

■ 304 Photo utilisée pour une affiche autopromotionnelle du photographe Chuck Shotwell. (USA)

■ 305 Autopromotion du photographe Sicco Kolff. (NLD)

PHOTOGRAPHER:
Sicco Kolff
STYLIST:
Sicco Kolff
DESIGNER:
Sicco Kolff
■ 305

PHOTOGRAPHER:
JODY DOLE
CLIENT:
RAPOPORT PRINTING CORP.
ART DIRECTOR:
JODY DOLE
■ 306

■ 306-308 From a still life with flowers series, shot by photographer Jody Dole of New York and used as self-promotion. *306* is a poster. (USA)

■ 306-308 Aus einer Serie von Stilleben mit Blumen, von dem Photographen Jody Dole, New York, als Eigenwerbung verwendet. *306* ist ein Plakat. (USA)

■ 306-308 Photos d'une série de natures mortes aux fleurs que le photographe Jody Dole, de New York, utilise pour sa publicité personnelle. *306* est une affiche. (USA)

PHOTOGRAPHER:
JODY DOLE
ART DIRECTOR:
JODY DOLE
■ 307, 308

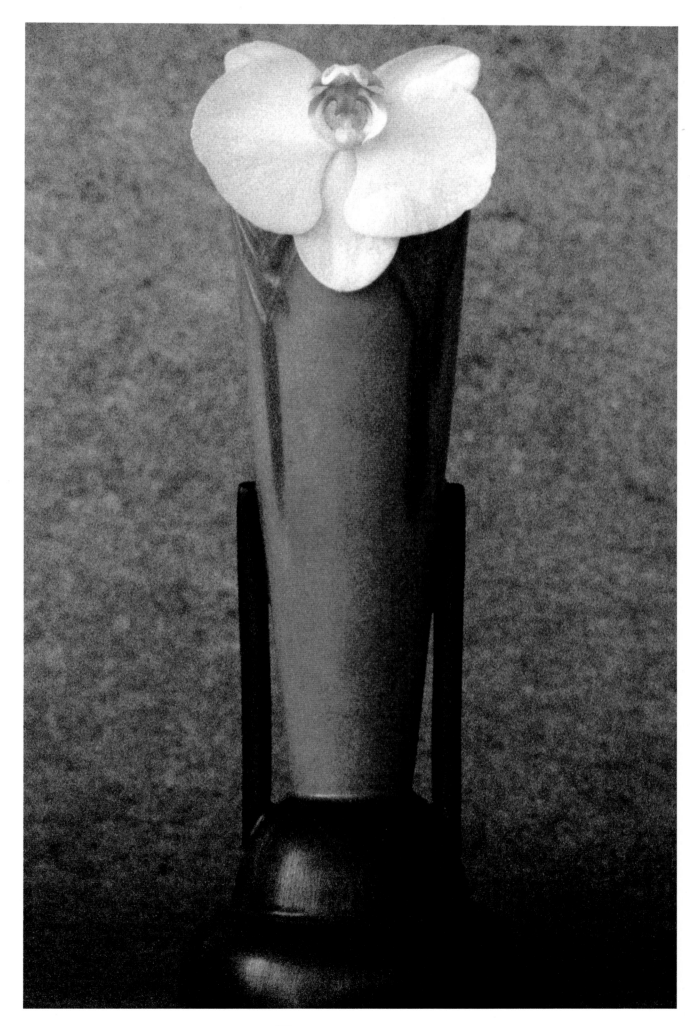

PHOTOGRAPHER:
PATIENCE ARAKAWA
CLIENT:
THE IMPERIAL HOTEL, TOKYO
ART DIRECTOR:
MICHAEL BARTON
DESIGNER:
KEIKO HON
AGENCY:
EMPHASIS! INC.
■ 309

■ 309 "Winter Dreams – Seasons pass but we remain."
Photograph for the Imperial Hotel, Tokyo. (JPN)

■ 309 «Winterträume – Jahreszeiten vergehen, aber wir
bleiben.» Aufnahme für das Imperial Hotel, Tokio. (JPN)

■ 309 «Rêves d'hiver – les saisons passent, nous restons.»
Photo pour l'Imperial Hotel de Tokyo. (JPN)

CUISINE

LEBENSMITTEL

PHOTOGRAPHER:
FRANÇOIS GILLET
CLIENT:
*THE DAI-ICHI MUTUAL LIFE
INSURANCE COMPANY*
ART DIRECTOR:
DAISUKE NAKATSUKA
DESIGNER:
MASATO ISOBE
AGENCY:
NAKATSUKA DAISUKE INC.
■ 310

PHOTOGRAPHER:
JOHN JAMES WOOD
►■ 311

■ 310 From a calendar of the Dai-Ichi Mutual Life Insurance Company entitled "Photo-Cubism". (JPN)

■ 311 Unpublished photograph taken by John James Wood for his own promotion. (CAN)

■ 310 Aus einem Kalender der Dai-Ichi-Versicherungsgesellschaft, mit dem Titel «Photo-Kubismus». (JPN)

■ 311 Unveröffentlichte Aufnahme, als Eigenwerbung des Photographen John James Wood verwendet. (CAN)

■ 310 Pour un calendrier de la compagnie d'assurance Dai-Ichi intitulé «Cubisme photographique». (JPN)

■ 311 Photo inédite que son auteur, le photographe John James Wood, utilise pour sa promotion personnelle. (CAN)

PHOTOGRAPHER:
KATHRYN KLEINMAN
STYLIST:
AMY NATHAN
PUBLISHER:
CHRONICLE BOOKS
DESIGNER:
JACQUELINE JONES
■ 312–317

■ 312–317 From a book entitled *Openers* by Amy Nathan, illustrated with photographs by Kathryn Kleinman and published by Chronical Books. *312, 313* are double spreads. *314–317:* Kid's Canapes, Checkerboard Canapes, Sardine Plate, Smoked Salmon with Cucumber Canapes. (USA)

■ 312–317 Aus dem Buch *Openers* (Vorspeisen) von Amy Nathan, mit Aufnahmen von Kathryn Kleinman, erschienen bei Chronicle Books. *312, 313* sind doppelseitige Aufnahmen. *314–317:* Canapés für Kinder, Schachbrett-Canapés, Sardinen-Teller, Canapés mit Rauchlachs und Gurke. (USA)

■ 312–317 Extraits de l'ouvrage *Openers* (Hors-d'œuvre) d'Amy Nathan, photos de Kathryn Kleinman, aux Editions Chronicle Books. Fig. *312, 313:* photos double page. Fig. *314–317:* Canapés pour enfants, canapés style échiquier, assiettes de sardines, canapés de saumon fumé. (USA)

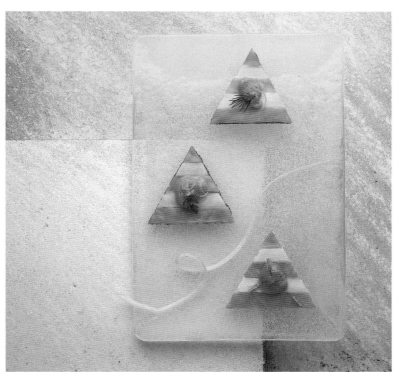

Photographer:
Kathryn Kleinman
Stylist:
Amy Nathan
Publisher:
Chronicle Books
Art Director:
Amy Nathan/
Kathryn Kleinman
Designer:
Jacqueline Jones
■ 318-322

■ 318-322 Examples of photographs from *Openers,* a cookbook on appetizers published by Chronicle Books. *318* shows an introductory page; *319-322* contain explanations and illustrations of the various ingredients and foods called for in the recipes. (USA)

■ 318-322 Beispiele der Aufnahmen aus dem Kochbuch *Openers* (Vorspeisen), das bei Chronicle Books erschienen ist. *318* wurde für eine einführende Seite verwendet, *319-322* sind mit Erklärungen zu den verschiedenen Nahrungsmitteln bzw. den dazugehörigen Rezepten versehen. (USA)

■ 318-322 Exemples des photos illustrant le livre de cuisine *Openers* (Hors-d'œuvre) paru aux Editions Chronicle Books. Fig. *318:* page initiale; fig. *319-322:* explications de divers plats respectivement des ingrédients que nécessite leur préparation. (USA)

PHOTOGRAPHER:
Tony Cenicola
DESIGNER:
Tony Cenicola
STUDIO:
Tony Cenicola
 323

PHOTOGRAPHER:
Jaume Blassi
CLIENT:
Cromoarte
ART DIRECTOR:
Jordi Blassi
DESIGNER:
Jordi Blassi
■ 324, 325

■ 323 Photograph taken by Tony Cenicola, New York, and used for his own promotion. (USA)

■ 323 Als Eigenwerbung verwendete Aufnahme des Photographen Tony Cenicola aus New York. (USA)

■ 323 Photo autopromotionnelle du photographe Tony Cenicola de New-York. (USA)

■ 324, 325 Personal studies by the photographer Jaume Blassi, Barcelona. (SPA)

■ 324, 325 Persönliche Studien des Photographen Jaume Blassi, Barcelona. (SPA)

■ 324, 325 Études personnelles du photographe Jaume Blassi de Barcelone. (SPA)

PHOTOGRAPHER:
WALTER SWARTHOUT
STYLIST:
WALTER SWARTHOUT
CLIENT:
SWARTHOUT & ASSOCIATES
ART DIRECTOR:
WALTER SWARTHOUT
DESIGNER:
MALCOLM E. BARKER
AGENCY:
SWARTHOUT & ASSOCIATES
■ 326

PHOTOGRAPHER:
STEVE MARSEL
CLIENT:
UNITED LITHOGRAPHY PRINTERS
ART DIRECTOR:
M.B. FLANDERS
DESIGNER:
M.B. FLANDERS
AGENCY:
FLANDERS AND ASSOCIATES
■ 327

PHOTOGRAPHER:
BERNHARD ANGERER
CLIENT:
A. DARBO GES.M.B.H.
ART DIRECTOR:
FRANZ MERLICEK
DESIGNER:
FRANZ HOCHWARTER
AGENCY:
DEMNER & MERLICEK
►■ 328

■ 326 For the cover of a brochure with photographs of foods used by the photographer Walter Swarthout for his own promotion. (USA)

■ 327 New Zealand Green Lip mussels from a promotional calendar published by United Lithography Printers. (USA)

■ 328 Ad intended for the gastronomic profession, publicizing *Darbo Naturrein* jams and jellies. (AUT)

■ 326 Für den Umschlag einer Eigenwerbungsbroschüre mit Nahrungsmittelaufnahmen des Photographen Walter Swarthout. (USA)

■ 327 Neuseeländische Muscheln, aus einer Werbe-Agenda der United Lithography Printers. (USA)

■ 328 Aus einer Anzeige, die sich an die Gastronomie richtet und für *Darbo-Naturrein*-Konfitüren wirbt. (AUT)

■ 326 Couverture d'une brochure autopromotionnelle du photographe Walter Swarthout (photos de produits alimentaires). (USA)

■ 327 Moules néo-zélandaises, dans un agenda publicitaire de United Lithography Printers. (USA)

■ 328 Pour une annonce destinée à l'hôtellerie en faveur des confitures sans additifs *Darbo Naturrein*. (AUT)

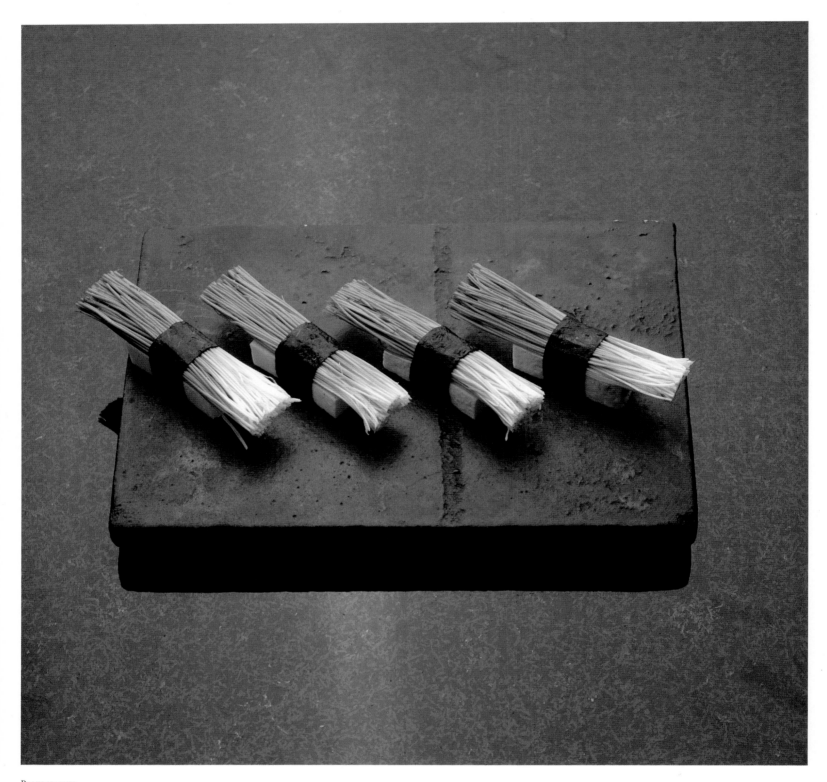

PHOTOGRAPHER:
REINHART WOLF
PUBLISHER:
RIZZOLI PUBLICATIONS
ART DIRECTOR:
CHARLES DAVEY
DESIGNER:
VILIM VASATE
AGENCY:
RIZZOLI INTERNATIONAL
PUBLICATIONS/IN-HOUSE
■ 329-338

■ 329–338 Examples of the full-page illustrations photographed by Reinhart Wolf for the book *Japan, the Beauty of Food*, published by Rizzoli, New York. (USA)

■ 329–338 Beispiele der ganzseitigen Aufnahmen aus dem Buch *Japan, The Beauty of Food* mit Aufnahmen von Reinhart Wolf, erschienen bei Rizzoli, New York. (USA)

■ 329–338 Exemples des photos pleine page illustrant l'album *Japan, The Beauty of Food* paru aux Editions Rizzoli de New York. Photos réalisées par Reinhart Wolf. (USA)

PHOTOGRAPHER:
REINHART WOLF
PUBLISHER:
RIZZOLI PUBLICATIONS
ART DIRECTOR:
CHARLES DAVEY
DESIGNER:
VILIM VASATE
AGENCY:
*RIZZOLI INTERNATIONAL
PUBLICATIONS/IN-HOUSE*
■ 339-346

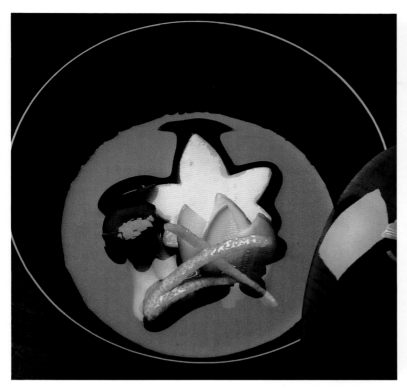

■ 339-346 Additional photographs (see *329-338)* from Reinhart Wolf's stunning pictorial of Japanese food styling. From *Japan, The Beauty of Food,* published by Rizzoli. (USA)

■ 339-346 Weitere Aufnahmen (s. *329-338),* in denen Reinhart Wolf die Schönheit japanischer Arrangements von Lebensmitteln zeigt. Aus *Japan, The Beauty of Food.* (USA)

■ 339-346 Photos où Reinhart Wolf dévoile la beauté des présentations japonaises de produits alimentaires (voir *329-338),*·dans *Japan, The Beauty of Food* (Rizzoli). (USA)

PHOTOGRAPHER:
Tobias Reymond
CLIENT:
Gist/Brocades
ART DIRECTOR:
Tobias Reymond
DESIGNER:
Tobias Reymond
AGENCY:
De Graaf & Pouvée
■ 347, 348

■ 347, 348 Photographs for an annual report and a calendar published by the firm Gist/Brocades. (NLD)

■ 347, 348 Aufnahmen für einen Jahresbericht und einen Kalender der Firma Gist/Brocades. (NLD)

■ 347, 348 Photos pour un rapport annuel et un calendrier de l'entreprise Gist/Brocades. (NLD)

■ 349-352 "Tomato", "Duck Egg", "Mocha", "Olive" – these are a few of the autumn colors figuratively presented in an advertisement for Galleria fashions. (USA)

■ 353 "A romantic dinner for two." Photograph for an article in *Food & Wine Magazine.* (USA)

■ 349-352 «Tomate», «Entenei», «Mokka», «Olive» – das sind einige der Herbstmodefarben, die in einer Anzeige für Galleria-Moden bildlich dargestellt sind. (USA)

■ 353 «Ein romantisches Abendessen für zwei.» Aufnahme für einen Beitrag im *Food & Wine Magazine.* (USA)

■ 349-352 «Tomate», «œuf de canard», «moka», «olive», ce sont des coloris d'automne nouveaux présentés entre autres dans une annonce des modes Galleria. (USA)

■ 353 «Souper romantique à deux.» Photo pour un article publié dans le *Food & Wine Magazine.* (USA)

PHOTOGRAPHER:
BUCK HOLTZMER
CLIENT:
GALLERIA MERCHANTS ASSOC.
ART DIRECTOR:
JAC COVERDALE
AGENCY:
CLARITY COVERDALE RUEFF
◄■ 349-352

PHOTOGRAPHER:
JERRY SIMPSON
PUBLISHER:
AMERICAN EXPRESS PUBLISHING CORP.
ART DIRECTOR:
ELIZABETH G. WOODSON
DESIGNER:
ELIZABETH G. WOODSON/ LORETTA SALA
STUDIO:
FOOD & WINE MAGAZINE
■ 353

■ 354-357 Personal studies by the photographer Karen Capucilli, New York. (USA)

■ 354-357 Persönliche Studien der Photographin Karen Capucilli, New York. (USA)

■ 354-357 Études personnelles de la photographe Karen Capucilli de New York. (USA)

PHOTOGRAPHER:
KAREN CAPUCILLI
■ 354-357

■ 354-357 Personal studies by the photographer Karen Capucilli, New York. (USA)

■ 354-357 Persönliche Studien der Photographin Karen Capucilli, New York. (USA)

■ 354-357 Études personnelles de la photographe Karen Capucilli de New York. (USA)

PHOTOGRAPHER:
RON CROFOOT
CLIENT:
CROFOOT PHOTOGRAPHY
ART DIRECTOR:
RON CROFOOT
DESIGNER:
WAYNE TALLEY
◄■ 358

PHOTOGRAPHER:
JERRY SIMPSON
STYLIST:
LINDA CHEVERTON/
ANNE DISRUDE
PUBLISHER:
AMERICAN EXPRESS
PUBLISHING CORP.
ART DIRECTOR:
ELIZABETH G. WOODSON
DESIGNER:
ELIZABETH G. WOODSON
STUDIO:
FOOD & WINE MAGAZINE
■ 359

■ 358 Photograph for the front page of a self-promotional folder of the Crofoot Photo Studio, Minneapolis. (USA)

■ 359 From an article in *Food & Wine Magazine* entitled "The New Crop of Fruits and Vegetables". (USA)

■ 358 Aufnahme für die Vorderseite einer Eigenwerbungsmappe des Photostudios Crofoot, Minneapolis. (USA)

■ 359 Aus einem Beitrag im *Food & Wine Magazine:* «Die neue Ernte von Früchten und Gemüse.» (USA)

■ 358 Photo pour la couverture d'un portfolio autopromotionnel du studio de photo Crofoot de Minneapolis. (USA)

■ 359 Pour un article du *Food & Wine Magazine* sur «La nouvelle récolte de fruits et légumes.» (USA)

PHOTOGRAPHER:
BILL WHITE
■ 360

■ 360 Unpublished photo-
graph taken by the New
York photographer Bill
White. (USA)

■ 360 Unveröffentlichte Aufnahme des New Yorker Pho-
tographen Bill White. (USA)

■ 360 Photo inédite du
photographe new-yorkais
Bill White. (USA)

VERZEICHNIS

GRAPHIS DESIGN

ALL ENTRIES MUST ARRIVE ON OR BEFORE NOVEMBER 30

Advertising: Newspaper and magazine.
Design: Promotion brochures, catalogs, invitations, record covers, announcements, logotypes and/or entire corporate image campaigns, calendars, books, book covers, packages (single or series, labels and/or complete packages)
Editorial Design: company magazines, newspapers, consumer magazines, house organs
Illustration: All categories may be black and white or color

GRAPHIS ANNUAL REPORTS

ALL ENTRIES MUST ARRIVE ON OR BEFORE JANUARY 31

All material printed and published in connection with the annual report of a company or other organization.
Design, illustration, photography, typography, as well as the overall conception of the annual report are the criteria to be judged.
In order to do justice to this complex medium, we will present double-page spreads from the annual reports selected which are exemplary in their design and/or illustration.

GRAPHIS PHOTO

ALL ENTRIES MUST ARRIVE ON OR BEFORE JUNE 30

Advertising Photography: Advertisements, promotional brochures, catalogs, invitations, announcements, record covers, calendars.
Editorial Photography for press media – journalism and features – for books, corporate publications, etc. on the following subjects: fashion, cosmetics, architecture, arts, nature, science, technology, daily life, sports, current affairs, portraits, still life, etc.
Fine Art Photography: Personal studies
Unpublished Photography: Experimental and student work

GRAPHIS POSTER

ALL ENTRIES MUST ARRIVE ON OR BEFORE APRIL 30

Culture: Posters announcing exhibitions and events of all kind, film, theater, and ballet performances, concerts etc.
Advertising: Posters for fashion, cosmetics, foods, beverages, industrial goods; image and self-promotional campaigns of companies and individuals
Society: Posters which serve primarily a social and/or political purpose; from the field of education; for conferences and meetings; as well as for political and charitable appeals.

GENERAL RULES

THESE ARE APPLICABLE TO ALL BOOKS MENTIONED.

By submitting work to GRAPHIS, the sender expressly grants permission for his publication in any GRAPHIS book, as well as in any article in GRAPHIS magazine, or any advertising brochure, etc. whose purpose is specifically to promote the sales of these publications.

Eligibility: All work produced in the 12 month period previous to the submission deadlines, as well as rejected or unpublished work from this period, by professionals and students.

A confirmation of receipt will be sent to each entrant, and all entrants will be notified at a later date whether or not their work has been accepted for publication. All the winning entries will be reproduced in a generous format and in four colors throughout.
By submitting work you qualify for a 25% discount on the purchase of the respective book.

What to send:
Please send the actual printed piece (unmounted but well protected). Do not send original art. For large, bulky or valuable pieces, please submit color photos or (duplicate) transparencies.
Please note that entries cannot be returned. Only in exceptional cases and by contacting us in advance will material be sent back.

Entry Fees:
For each single entry: North America: US$ 10.00 West Germany: DM 10,00 All other countries: SFr. 10.00
For each campaign entry of 3 or more pieces: North America: US$ 25.00 West Germany: DM 25,00 All other countries: SFr. 25.00
Please make checks payable to GRAPHIS PRESS CORP. Zurich, and include in parcel. These fees do not apply to students, if copy of student identification is included. (For entries from countries with exchange controls, please contact us.)

How and where to send:
Please tape (do not glue) the entry label provided (or photocopy) – with full information – on the back of each piece. Entries can be sent by airmail, air parcel post or surface mail. **Please do not send anything by air freight.** Declare "No Commercial Value" on packages, and label "Art for Contest". The number of transparencies and photos should be indicated on the parcel. (If sent by air courier, please mark "Documents, Commercial Value 00.00").

Thank you for your contribution. Please send all entries to the following address:
GRAPHIS PRESS CORP., DUFOURSTRASSE 107, CH-8008 ZURICH, SWITZERLAND

FÜR DIE GRAPHIS JAHRBÜCHER

GRAPHIS DESIGN

EINSENDESCHLUSS: 30. NOVEMBER

Werbung: In Zeitungen und Zeitschriften
Design: Werbeprospekte, Kataloge, Einladungen, Schallplattenhüllen, Anzeigen, Signete und/oder Imagekampagnen, Kalender, Bücher, Buchumschläge, Packungen (einzelne oder Serien, Etiketten und/oder vollständige Packungen)
Redaktionelles Design: Firmenpublikationen, Zeitungen, Zeitschriften, Jahresberichte
Illustration: Alle Kategorien, schwarzweiss oder farbig

GRAPHIS ANNUAL REPORTS

EINSENDESCHLUSS: 31. JANUAR

Alle gedruckten und veröffentlichten Arbeiten, die im Zusammenhang mit dem Jahresbericht einer Firma oder Organisation stehen.
Design, Illustration, Photographie, Typographie und die Gesamtkonzeption eines Jahresberichtes sind die beurteilten Kriterien.
Um diesem komplexen Medium gerecht zu werden, werden aus den ausgewählten Jahresberichten verschiedene typische Doppelseiten gezeigt, die beispielhaft für die Gestaltung und/oder Illustration sind.

GRAPHIS PHOTO

EINSENDESCHLUSS: 30. JUNI

Werbephotographie: Anzeigen, Prospekte, Kataloge, Einladungen, Bekanntmachungen, Schallplattenhüllen, Kalender.
Redaktionelle Photographie für Presse (Reportagen und Artikel), Bücher, Firmenpublikationen usw. in den Bereichen Mode, Kosmetik, Architektur, Kunst, Natur, Wissenschaft und Technik, Alltag, Sport, Aktuelles, Porträts, Stilleben usw.
Künstlerische Photographie: Persönliche Studien
Unveröffentlichte Aufnahmen: Experimentelle Photographie und Arbeiten von Studenten und Schülern.

GRAPHIS POSTER

EINSENDESCHLUSS: 30. APRIL

Kultur: Plakate für die Ankündigung von Ausstellungen und Veranstaltungen aller Art, Film-, Theater- und Ballettaufführungen, Musikveranstaltungen.
Werbung: Plakate für Mode, Kosmetik, Lebensmittel, Genussmittel, Industriegüter; Image- und Eigenwerbung von Firmen und Einzelpersonen
Gesellschaft: Plakate, die in erster Linie einem sozialen oder politischen Zweck dienen, auf dem Gebiet der Ausbildung und Erziehung oder für die Ankündigung von Konferenzen und Tagungen sowie für politische und soziale Appelle

TEILNAHMEBEDINGUNGEN

DIESE GELTEN FÜR ALLE AUFGEFÜHRTEN BÜCHER.

Durch Ihre Einsendung geben Sie GRAPHIS ausdrücklich die Erlaubnis zur Veröffentlichung der eingesandten Arbeiten sowohl im entsprechenden Jahrbuch als auch in der Zeitschrift GRAPHIS oder für die Wiedergabe im Zusammenhang mit Besprechungen und Werbematerial für die GRAPHIS-Publikationen.

In Frage kommen alle Arbeiten von Fachleuten und Studenten – auch nicht publizierte Arbeiten – welche in den zwölf Monaten vor Einsendeschluss entstanden sind.

Jeder Einsender erhält eine Empfangsbestätigung und wird über Erscheinen oder Nichterscheinen seiner Arbeiten zu einem späteren Zeitpunkt informiert.
Alle im Buch aufgenommenen Arbeiten werden vierfarbig, in grosszügigem Format reproduziert.
Durch Ihre Einsendung erhalten Sie 25% Rabatt auf das jeweilige Jahrbuch.

Was einsenden:
Bitte senden Sie uns das gedruckte Beispiel (unmontiert, aber gut geschützt).
Senden Sie keine Originale. Bei unhandlichen, umfangreichen oder wertvollen Sendungen bitten wir um Farbphotos oder Duplikat-Dias.
Bitte beachten Sie, dass Einsendungen nicht zurückgeschickt werden können. Ausnahmen sind nur nach vorheriger Absprache mit GRAPHIS möglich.

Gebühren:
SFr. 10.00/DM 10,00 für einzelne Arbeiten
SFr. 25.00/DM 25,00 für Kampagnen oder Serien von mehr als drei Stück
Bitte senden Sie uns einen Scheck (SFr.-Schecks bitte auf eine Schweizer Bank ziehen) oder überweisen Sie den Betrag auf PC Zürich 80-23071-9 oder PSchK Frankfurt 3000 57-602.
Diese Gebühren gelten nicht für Studenten. Bitte schicken Sie uns eine Kopie des Studentenausweises.
(Für Einsendungen aus Ländern mit Devisenbeschränkungen bitten wir Sie, uns zu kontaktieren.)

Wie und wohin schicken:
Bitte befestigen Sie das vorgesehene Etikett (oder eine Kopie) – vollständig ausgefüllt – mit Klebstreifen (nicht mit Klebstoff) auf der Rückseite jeder Arbeit. Bitte per Luftpost oder auf normalem Postweg einsenden. **Keine Luftfrachtsendungen.** Deklarieren Sie «Ohne jeden Handelswert» und «Arbeitsproben für Wettbewerb». Die Anzahl der Dias und Photos sollte auf dem Paket angegeben werden. (Bei Air Courier Sendungen vermerken Sie «Dokumente, ohne jeden Handelswert»).

Herzlichen Dank für Ihre Mitarbeit. Bitte senden Sie Ihre Arbeiten an folgende Adresse:
GRAPHIS VERLAG AG, DUFOURSTRASSE 107, CH-8008 ZURICH, SCHWEIZ

267

G R A P H I S   D E S I G N

DATE LIMITE D'ENVOI: 30 NOVEMBRE

Publicité: journaux et magazines
Design: brochures de promotion, catalogues, invitations, pochettes de disques, annonces, emblèmes, en-têtes, campagnes de prestige, calendriers, livres, jaquettes, emballages (spécimen ou série, étiquettes ou emballages complets)
Editorial Design: magazines de sociétés, journaux, revues, rapports annuels
Illustration: toutes catégories en noir et blanc ou en couleurs

G R A P H I S   A N N U A L   R E P O R T S

DATE LIMITE D'ENVOI: 31 JANVIER

Tous travaux imprimés et publiés en relation avec le rapport annuel d'une entreprise ou d'une organisation.
Les critères retenus pour l'appréciation sont le design, l'illustration, la photo, la typo et la conception d'ensemble des rapports annuels.
Afin de rendre justice à ce média complexe, nous présentons diverses doubles pages types des rapports annuels sélectionnés en veillant à ce qu'elles soient représentatives de la conception et/ou de l'illustration.

G R A P H I S   P H O T O

DATE LIMITE D'ENVOI: 30 JUIN

Photographie publicitaire: annonces, brochures de promotion, catalogues, invitations, pochettes de disques, calendriers
Photographie rédactionnelle pour la presse (reportages et articles), livres, publications d'entreprises, etc. dans les domaines suivants: Mode, arts, architecture, nature, sciences et techniques, vie quotidienne, sports, l'actualité, portraits, nature morte, etc.
Photographie artistique: études personnelles
Photographie non publiée: travaux expérimentaux et projets d'étudiants

G R A P H I S   P O S T E R

DATE LIMITE D'ENVOI: 30 AVRIL

Affiches culturelles: annonçant des expositions et manifestations de tout genre, des projections de films, des représentations de théâtre et de ballet, des concerts et festivals.
Affiches publicitaires: pour la mode, les cosmétiques, l'alimentation, les produits de consommation de luxe, les biens industriels; publicité institutionnelle et auto-promotion d'entreprises.
Affiches sociales: essentiellement au service d'une cause sociale ou politique dans les domaines de l'éducation et de la formation, ainsi que pour l'annonce de conférences et réunions et pour les appels à caractère social et politique.

M O D A L I T É S   D ' E N V O I

VALABLES POUR TOUS LES LIVRES CITÉS.

Par votre envoi, vous donnez expressément à GRAPHIS l'autorisation de reproduire les travaux reçus aussi bien dans le livre en question que dans le magazine GRAPHIS ou dans tout imprimé relatif aux comptes rendus et au matériel publicitaire concernant les publications GRAPHIS.

Sont acceptés tous les travaux de professionnels et d'étudiants – même inédits – réalisés pendant les douze mois précédant le délai limite d'envoi.

Pour tout envoi de travaux, nous vous faisons parvenir un accusé de réception. Vous serez informé par la suite de la parution ou non-parution de vos travaux. Tous les travaux figurant dans l'ouvrage en question sont reproduits en quadrichromie dans un format généreux.
Votre envoi vous vaut une réduction de 25% sur l'annuel en question.

Que nous envoyer:
Veuillez nous envoyer un exemplaire imprimé (non monté, mais bien protégé). N'envoyez pas d'originaux. Pour les travaux de grand format, volumineux ou de valeur, veuillez nous envoyer des photos ou des diapositives (duplicata). **Veuillez noter que les travaux ne peuvent pas être retournés,** sauf dans des cas exceptionnels et si vous nous en avisez à l'avance.

Droits d'admission:
SFr. 10.00 pour les envois concernant un seul travail
SFr. 25.00 pour chaque série de 3 travaux ou davantage
Veuillez joindre à votre envoi un chèque tiré sur une banque suisse ou en verser le montant au compte chèque postal Zürich 80-23071-9.
Les étudiants sont exemptés de cette taxe. Prière de joindre une photocopie de la carte d'étudiant.
(Si vous résidez dans un pays qui connaît le contrôle des changes, veuillez nous contacter préalablement.)

Comment et où envoyer:
Veuillez scotcher (ne pas coller) au dos de chaque spécimen les étiquettes ci-jointes (ou photocopies) – dûment remplies. Envoyez les travaux de préférence par avion, ou par voie de surface. **Ne nous envoyez rien en fret aérien.** Indiquez «Sans aucune valeur commerciale» et «Echantillons de spécimens pour concours». Le nombre de diapositives et de photos doit être indiqué sur le paquet. (Pour les envois par courrier, inscrire «Documents, sans aucune valeur commercial».)

Nous vous remercions chaleureusement de votre collaboration. Veuillez faire parvenir vos travaux à l'adresse suivante:

EDITIONS GRAPHIS SA, DUFOURSTRASSE 107, CH-8008 ZURICH, SUISSE

ENTRY LABEL

Please tape (do not glue) this label or a photocopy to the back of each entry.

SENDER:
Firm, Address, Telephone

ART DIRECTOR:
Name, City, State

DESIGNER:
Name, City, State

ILLUSTRATOR, PHOTOGRAPHER:
Name, City, State

STYLIST:
Name, City, State

COPYWRITER:
Name, City, State

AGENCY, STUDIO:
Name, City, State

CLIENT, PUBLISHER:
Complete address

DESCRIPTION OF ASSIGNMENT/OTHER INFORMATION:

■ I herewith grant GRAPHIS PRESS non-exclusive permission for use of the submitted material, for which I have full reproduction rights (copy, photography, illustration, and design)

SIGNATURE:

ETIKETT/FICHE

Bitte auf der Rückseite jeder Arbeit befestigen/veuillez scotcher au dos de chaque spécimen.

ABSENDER/ENVOYÉ PAR:
Firma(e), Adresse, Telephon(e)

ART DIRECTOR/DIRECTEUR ARTISTIQUE:
Name, Ort/Nom, Lieu

GESTALTER/DESIGNER:
Name, Ort/Nom, Lieu

KÜNSTLER/ARTISTE, PHOTOGRAPH(E):
Name, Ort/Nom, Lieu

STYLIST/STYLISTE:
Name, City, State

TEXTER/RÉDACTEUR:
Name, Ort/Nom, Lieu

AGENTUR/AGENCE:
Name, Ort/Nom, Lieu

KUNDE/CLIENT:
Adresse

ZWECK/UTILISATION:
INFORMATION:

■ Ich erteile hiermit dem GRAPHIS VERLAG die nicht-exklusive Erlaubnis zur Veröffentlichung der eingereichten Arbeiten, für die ich die Reproduktionsrechte besitze (Text, Photographie, Illustration und Design).

■ J'accorde par la présente aux EDITIONS GRAPHIS l'autorisation non exclusive d'utiliser le matériel soumis à leur appréciation, pour lequel je détiens les droits de reproduction (texte, photographie, illustration et design).

UNTERSCHRIFT/
SIGNATURE:

ADDRESS LABEL

GRAPHIS PRESS CORP.
107 DUFOURSTRASSE
CH-8008 ZURICH
SWITZERLAND

ADDRESS LABEL

GRAPHIS PRESS CORP.
107 DUFOURSTRASSE
CH-8008 ZURICH
SWITZERLAND

SUBSCRIBE TO GRAPHIS: FOR USA AND CANADA

MAGAZINE	USA	CANADA
☐ GRAPHIS (One year/6 issues)	US$ 59.00	CDN$ 82.00
☐ 1987 Portfolio (Case holds six issues)	US$ 11.00	CDN$ 15.00

☐ Check enclosed
☐ Please bill me (My subscription will begin upon payment)
☐ Students may request a 25% discount by sending student ID.
IMPORTANT! PLEASE CHECK THE LANGUAGE VERSION DESIRED:
☐ ENGLISH ☐ GERMAN ☐ FRENCH

NAME

TITLE

COMPANY

ADDRESS

CITY

STATE/PROV.   POSTAL CODE

COUNTRY

PROFESSION

SIGNATURE   DATE

Please send coupon and make check payable to:
GRAPHIS US, INC., 141 LEXINGTON AVENUE, NEW YORK, NY 10016, USA.
Guarantee: You may cancel your subscription at any time and receive a full refund on all
unmailed copies. Please allow 6–8 weeks for delivery of first issue.

REQUEST FOR CALL FOR ENTRIES

Please put me on your "Call for Entries" list for the following title(s).
Please check the appropriate box(es).
☐ GRAPHIS PHOTO ☐ GRAPHIS POSTER ☐ GRAPHIS DESIGN
☐ GRAPHIS PACKAGING ☐ GRAPHIS DIAGRAM ☐ GRAPHIS ANNUAL REPORTS
By submitting material to any of the titles listed above, I will automatically qualify for a
25% discount toward the purchase of the title.   PG 89

SUBSCRIBE TO GRAPHIS: FOR EUROPE AND THE WORLD

MAGAZINE	BRD	WORLD	U.K.
☐ GRAPHIS (One year/6 issues)	DM 156,–	SFr. 126.–	£ 48.00
☐ 1987 Portfolio (Case holds six issues)	DM 24.–	SFr. 19.–	£ 8.00

☐ Check enclosed (for Europe, please make SFr.-checks payable to a Swiss bank)
☐ Please bill me (My subscription will begin upon payment)
☐ Students may request a 25% discount by sending student ID.
IMPORTANT! PLEASE CHECK THE LANGUAGE VERSION DESIRED:
☐ ENGLISH ☐ GERMAN ☐ FRENCH
Subscription fees include postage to any part of the world.
Airmail Surcharges: SFr. 12.00 / DM 14,00 / £ 4.50 for Europe
       SFr. 50.00 / DM 60,00 / £ 20.00 for Africa/Asia/Latin America
       SFr. 65.00 / DM 78,00 / £ 25.00 for Australia/Pacific
Registered Mail: SFr. 13.00 / DM 15,00 / £ 5.25 (Recommended for Latin America/India)

NAME

TITLE

COMPANY

ADDRESS

CITY   POSTAL CODE

COUNTRY

PROFESSION

SIGNATURE   DATE

Please send coupon and make check payable to:
GRAPHIS PRESS CORP., DUFOURSTRASSE 107, CH-8008 ZÜRICH, SWITZERLAND
Guarantee: You may cancel your subscription at any time and receive a full refund on all
unmailed copies. Please allow 6–8 weeks for delivery of first issue.

REQUEST FOR CALL FOR ENTRIES

Please put me on your "Call for Entries" list for the following title(s).
Please check the appropriate box(es).
☐ GRAPHIS PHOTO ☐ GRAPHIS POSTER ☐ GRAPHIS DESIGN
☐ GRAPHIS PACKAGING ☐ GRAPHIS DIAGRAM ☐ GRAPHIS ANNUAL REPORTS
By submitting material to any of the titles listed above, I will automatically qualify for a
25% discount toward the purchase of the title.   PG 89

BOOK ORDER FORM: FOR USA AND CANADA

ORDER YOUR GRAPHIS ANNUALS NOW!

BOOKS	USA	CANADA
☐ Graphis Photo 89	US$ 65.00	CDN$ 98.00
☐ Graphis Poster 89	US$ 65.00	CDN$ 98.00
☐ Graphis Packaging 5	US$ 75.00	CDN$ 105.00
☐ Graphis Design 89	US$ 65.00	CDN$ 98.00
☐ Graphis Photo 88	US$ 65.00	CDN$ 98.00
☐ Graphis Diagram 1	US$ 65.00	CDN$ 98.00
☐ Graphis Annual Reports 1	US$ 65.00	CDN$ 98.00
☐ Graphis Poster 88	US$ 65.00	CDN$ 98.00
☐ 42 Years of Graphis Covers (1944–1986)	US$ 49.50	CDN$ 60.00

☐ Check enclosed
☐ Please bill me (Mailing costs in addition to above book price will be charged)

NAME

TITLE

COMPANY

ADDRESS

CITY/STATE/PROV.

POSTAL CODE   COUNTRY

PROFESSION

SIGNATURE   DATE

Please send coupon and make check payable to:
GRAPHIS US, INC., 141 LEXINGTON AVENUE, NEW YORK, NY 10016, USA.

REQUEST FOR CALL FOR ENTRIES

Please put me on your "Call for Entries" list for the following title(s).
Please check the appropriate box(es).
☐ GRAPHIS PHOTO ☐ GRAPHIS POSTER ☐ GRAPHIS DESIGN
☐ GRAPHIS PACKAGING ☐ GRAPHIS DIAGRAM ☐ GRAPHIS ANNUAL REPORTS
By submitting material to any of the titles listed above, I will automatically qualify for a
25% discount toward the purchase of the title.   PG 89

BOOK ORDER FORM: FOR EUROPE AND THE WORLD

BOOKS	BRD	WORLD	U.K.
☐ Graphis Photo 89	DM 148,–	SFr. 118.–	£ 46.50
☐ Graphis Poster 89	DM 148,–	SFr. 118.–	£ 46.50
☐ Graphis Packaging 5	DM 160,–	SFr. 132.–	£ 48.00
☐ Graphis Design 89	DM 138,–	SFr. 112.–	£ 45.00
☐ Graphis Photo 88	DM 138,–	SFr. 112.–	£ 45.00
☐ Graphis Diagram 1	DM 138,–	SFr. 112.–	£ 45.00
☐ Graphis Annual Reports 1	DM 138,–	SFr. 112.–	£ 45.00
☐ Graphis Poster 88	DM 138,–	SFr. 112.–	£ 45.00
☐ 42 Years of Graphis Covers (1944–1986)	DM 98,–	SFr. 85.–	£ 35.00

☐ Check enclosed (For Europe, please make SFr. checks payable to a Swiss Bank)
☐ Amount paid into Graphis account at the Union Bank of Switzerland, Acct No 3620063
in Zürich.
☐ Amount paid to Postal Cheque Account Zürich 80-23071-9 (Through your local post office)
☐ Please bill me (Mailing costs in addition to above book price will be charged)

NAME

TITLE

COMPANY

ADDRESS

CITY   POSTAL CODE

COUNTRY

PROFESSION

SIGNATURE   DATE

Please send coupon and make check payable to:
GRAPHIS PRESS CORP., DUFOURSTRASSE 107, CH-8008 ZÜRICH, SWITZERLAND

REQUEST FOR CALL FOR ENTRIES

Please put me on your "Call for Entries" list for the following title(s).
Please check the appropriate box(es).
☐ GRAPHIS PHOTO ☐ GRAPHIS POSTER ☐ GRAPHIS DESIGN
☐ GRAPHIS PACKAGING ☐ GRAPHIS DIAGRAM ☐ GRAPHIS ANNUAL REPORTS
By submitting material to any of the titles listed above, I will automatically qualify for a
25% discount toward the purchase of the title.   PG 89

GRAPHIS PRESS CORP.
DUFOURSTRASSE 107
CH-8008 ZÜRICH
SWITZERLAND

GRAPHIS U.S., INC.
141 LEXINGTON AVENUE
NEW YORK, NEW YORK 10016
U.S.A.

GRAPHIS PRESS CORP.
DUFOURSTRASSE 107
CH-8008 ZÜRICH
SWITZERLAND

GRAPHIS U.S., INC.
141 LEXINGTON AVENUE
NEW YORK, NEW YORK 10016
U.S.A.